Sanskrit Inscriptions of Tamil Nadu
A Literary Study

Sanskrit Inscriptions of Tamil Nadu

A Literary Study

Charu Madhavan

SHARADA

Sharada Publishing House

Delhi - 110 085

2007

First Published : 2007

ISBN : 81-88934-41-0

Published by
B.L. Bansal
SHARADA PUBLISHING HOUSE
(Publishers on India's Past and Present)
111, Vidya Vihar Aptt., Sector-9,
Rohini, Delhi-110085
Ph. : 011-32921560, 27552102
Email : bansal_sph@rediffmail.com

Laser Typesetting by
Creative Graphics

Printed at
Salasar Imaging Systems, Delhi-110035

Dedicated to

The poet-composers of the Sanskrit inscriptions of the
Pallava, Pāṇḍya and Chōḷa ages
and to the pioneering Sanskrit epigraphists

Contents

Preface

This book embodies the result of the research carried out by me from 2001-2003 as a recipient of the Senior Fellowship in Epigraphy, Government of India.

I am immensely grateful to Dr. K.V. Raman, Former Prof. and Head, Department of Ancient History and Archaeology, University of Madras, for suggesting this topic to me and for his valuable suggestions and encouragement at every stage of my research work.

I sincerely thank Dr. Srikantha Sarma, Lecturer, Madras Sanskrit College, Chennai for all the help he has rendered to me during the period of this research work. I thank my family for their support and constant encouragement. My special thanks to my daughter, Dr. Chithra Madhavan for helping me at every stage of my research work.

I wholeheartedly thank Shri B.L. Bansal of Sharada Publishing House for the interest and enthusiasm he has shown in bringing out this book.

Charu Madhavan

Abbreviations

ALB	:	Adyar Library Bulletin
ARE	:	Annual Reports of Epigraphy
DCVP	:	Daḷavāypuram Copper-plate Grant of Parāntaka Vīra-Nārāyaṇa Pāṇḍya by T.N. Subrahmaniam
E.I.	:	Epigraphia Indica
ECPR	:	Esalam Copper-plates of Rājēndra Chōḷa I by R. Nagaswamy
I.A.	:	Indian Antiquary
KTPR	:	Karandai Tamil Sangam Plates of Rājēndra Chōḷa I by K.G. Krishnan
PCM	:	Pāṇḍiar Ceppetukal Pattu
SCVP	:	Śivakāsī Copper-plate grant of Vīra-Pāṇḍya by T.N. Subrahmaniam and P.R. Srinivasan
S.I.I.	:	South Indian Inscriptions
S.I.T.I.	:	South Indian Temple Inscriptions
TAS	:	Travancore Archaeological Series
TVCP	:	Tiruttani and Vēḷāñjēri Copper-plates by R. Nagaswamy

Method of Transliteration

The method adopted in this book for transliterating the Sanskrit words is the same as that followed in the publications of the Archaeological Survey of India such as Epigraphia Indica and South Indian Inscriptions.

Introduction

Of all the sources for writing about the history of ancient India, namely numismatics, epigraphy, legends and folklore, the study of inscriptions or epigraphy is the most important one as these epigraphs provide copious and authentic data about various aspects of life in the ancient period.

The inscriptions discovered in different parts of India are found written in different languages, but a majority of them are composed in Sanskrit as it was the court language of many of the ruling dynasties of ancient India and was widely understood across the length and breadth of this subcontinent. An indepth analysis of these Sanskrit epigraphs, both lithic as well as those found inscribed on copper-plate charters reveals that they serve not only as sources for knowing about the administrative, economic, social and cultural conditions of those times, but also reveal the standard and style of this language in the different periods. According to A.A. Macdonell, 'The inscriptions are important in connection with Sanskrit literature as illustrating both the early history of Indian writing and the state of the language at that time.'[1]

Many of the epigraphs of the rulers of ancient South India are composed in Sanskrit. In the ancient Tamil country, the rulers of the imperial dynasties of the Pallavas, Pāṇḍyas and Chōḷas gave innumerable gifts of money, jewels and land to the temples and also to the religious and scholarly brahmāṇas. These royal benefactions were recorded by way of inscriptions (*rāja-śāsanās*) on the walls of the temples or on copper-plate grants (*tāmra-śāsanās*) in accordance with the rules laid down in the *Dharmaśāstras*. A very large number of such epigraphs of the ancient Tamil country, which are actually royal documents, were written in the Sanskrit language.

The earliest inscriptions of the Pallava dynasty which ruled from its capital city Kāñchīpuram (Kāñchīpuram district, Tamil Nadu) were discovered in the Guntur, Kurnul, Bellary and Nellore districts of Andhra Pradesh. The earliest of these epigraphs namely, the Mañchikallu,[2] Maidavōlu,[3] Hiragadagalli[4] and the British Museum plates (Guṇapadēya plates) of Chārudēvī[5] were written in Prakrit. Later on, the Pallava inscriptions both lithic and copper-plates, were composed in Sanskrit. However, there are also a large number of copper-plate charters of the Pallava kings which are bi-lingual, i.e. written in Sanskrit and in the local language, Tamil. The introductory portion, called *praśasti* of these documents which narrate the genealogy of the rulers and their achievements is in Sanskrit verse or prose and the operative portion of the record which gives the details of the grant proper, be it a gift to a temple or a land-grant to brāhmaṇas, is in Tamil.

The Pāṇḍya dynasty too which ruled from Madurai issued a large number of epigraphs in Tamil and in Sanskrit and many of their copper-plate charters like the Vēḷvikuḍi,[6] Śrīvaramaṅgalam,[7] Siṉṉamaṉūr,[8] Daḷavāypuram[9] and Śivakāśi[10] copper-plate charters are bi-lingual with the first part in Sanskrit and the latter portion in Tamil. It is interesting to note that one of the early Pāṇḍyan epigraphs belonging to the 7th century A.D. of king Chēndan, written in Tamil contains numerous Sanskrit expressions to describe this king.[11] The style of this passage is reminiscent of the later Maṇipravāḷa used so profusely by the Śrī Vaishṇava commentators of the *Nālālyira-Divyaprabandham* and may be considered to be the earliest specimen of this style.[12] Many of these inscriptions also contain Sanskrit terms found in the *Dharmaśāstras* and the equivalent Tamil terms have also been written.[13]

With regard to the dynasty of the imperial Chōḷas whose capital was Tañjāvūr and later Gaṅgaikoṇḍachōḷapuram and who have issued the maximum number of inscriptions among the rulers of the ancient Tamil country, there are also very many records which are either fully in Sanskrit or are bi-lingual like the Vēḷānjēri,[14] Anbil,[15] Larger Leiden,[16] Tiruvālaṅgāḍu,[17] Karandai,[18] Esālam[19] and Kanyākumarī[20] epigraphs.

The inscriptions of the kings of the Tamil country, especially the copper-plate grants, almost always begin with a few invocatory verses in praise of various Gods and Goddesses followed by the mythical ancestry beginning from the sun or the moon (Sūrya-vaṁśa or Chandra-vaṁśa) of the dynasty to which the inscription belongs and then give the list of historical personages of that dynasty and lastly the exploits of the ruler in whose reign the document was composed and the actual donation made by him.

These inscriptions of the periods of the Pallava, Pāṇḍya and Chōḷa rulers which are fully in Sanskrit or which have Sanskrit *praśasti* portions are masterpieces of poetry and prose. The historians and archaeologists who have studied and analyzed these records have culled out the historical details from them, but an indepth study of the literary beauty contained in these Sanskrit inscriptions of Tamil Nadu has not been attempted.

The main reason for my undertaking this work is to bring out these hitherto unknown masterpieces of Sanskrit literature to light. Ravikīrti the talented poet-composer of the famous Aihoḷe inscription[21] of the Chālukyan ruler Pulakēsin II compares himself to the famous Sanskrit composers Kālidāsa and Bhāravi in this epigraph. The poets of the inscriptions of the Tamil country were no less talented than Ravikīrti and their works in prose and poetry as revealed by the stone and copper-plate records, speak volumes of their talent, scholarship and skill.

These poets have employed a very large variety of metres in their poems. A number of *alaṅkāras* (rhetoric) have also been used which embellish their work. A detailed study of their inscriptions shows that they were very familiar with the Sanskrit works of ancient India like the two epics, the *Rāmāyaṇa*, and the *Mahābhārata* and also many of the *Purāṇas* as well as some classical Sanskrit texts such as the works of Kālidāsa and Bāṇa. In numerous inscriptions, the kings are frequently compared with the heroes of the epics. It can also be seen that the composers of these epigraphs have used passages or ideas from the ancient texts in their works. According to D.B. Diskalkar, 'the authors of the south Indian inscriptions were great students of Vedic and classical Sanskrit literature in all its branches and frequently borrowed ideas and even portions from them.'[22]

These epigraphs, some in the form of poems, some in prose and yet others in a mixture of prose and verse, in the *champu* style give the names of the poet-composers at the very end of the epigraphs along with some details about their family and educational qualifications. The role of the kings of the ancient Tamil country in promoting Sanskrit learning and culture by employing such talented composers for writing their official records is evident from a study of these inscriptions. Sometimes, generations of poets of certain scholarly families were patronized by the rulers for composing such royal edicts.

Apart from the Sanskrit inscriptions of the Tamil kings, many other Sanskrit epigraphs of kings from outside the Tamil country who ruled over Tamil Nadu in the ancient period are also found inscribed on the walls of many temples. The Sanskrit records of the Chēra ruler Ravivarman Kulaśēkhara (1299-1314 A.D.), many Hoysala rulers like Vīra Rāmanātha (1254-1295 A.D.) and Ballāla III (1291-1343 A.D.) also reveal the scholarship and talent of their court poets. But for these inscriptions preserved for hundreds of years on the walls of temples and on copper-plates, the works of these great composers would have vanished into oblivion. In the following pages, an attempt has been made to analyze the literary beauty of the Sanskrit inscriptions of ancient Tamil Nadu.

This work is divided into four chapters. The first deals with a detail study of the Sanskrit lithic and copper-plate inscriptions of the Pallavas. The different meters and *alaṅkāras* used in their inscriptions which are both in prose and in the form of poetry, the names and qualifications of the poets who composed them and the echoes seen in their works from other literary texts of ancient India are all analyzed in this chapter.

Chapter II deals with the epigraphs belonging to the Pāṇḍyan period. Although the Sanskrit inscriptions of this age are far less than those belonging to the Pallava times yet their records, mostly copper-plate grants, reflect the mastery which these poets had over the Sanskrit language and their skill in composing poems based on the achievements and glories of their patron-kings. The beautiful similes and metaphors found in these copper-plate poems have been highlighted.

The next chapter deals with the Sanskrit epigraphs of the Chōḷa period. Compared to the age of the Pallavas once again, their lithic and copper-plate records are fewer in number, but more than compensated for by the sheer length of these epigraphs. The Sanskrit sections of some of these inscriptions like the Karandai, Tiruvālaṅgāḍu and Kanyākumarī records are extremely long. Among the lithic records, an inscription of a Chōḷa general named Naralōka-vīra found in the famous Naṭarāja (Śiva) temple at Chidambaram is also lengthy. These records are examples of the high standard of Sanskrit learning during that period and reveal that such versatile poet-scholars lived in the Tamil land at that time.

The last chapter deals with the Sanskrit inscriptions of many of the vassal chiefs of these imperial powers who too employed many talented poets to compose their epigraphs and also the Sanskrit inscriptions of kings from the Kerala and Karnataka areas, mentioned earlier, who have left behind their epigraphs inscribed on the walls of various temples in Tamil Nadu to which they gifted land, money and jewels.

REFERENCES

1. Macdonell, A.A., *A History of Sanskrit Literature*, Delhi, 1979, p.12.
2. *E.I.*, Vol. XXXII, No. 2, pp. 89-90 (Mañchikallu inscription).
3. *E.I.*, Vol. VI, No. 8, pp. 87-88 (Maidavolu plates).
4. *E.I.*, Vol. I, No. I, pp. 5-6 (Hirahadagalli plates).
5. *E.I.*, Vol. VIII, No.12, pp. 145-146 (British Museum Plates of Chārudēvī).
6. *E.I.*, XVII, No 16. pp. 298-304 (Vēlvikuḍi plates).
7. *PCP*, pp. 56-57.
8. *S.I.I.*, Vol. III, No. 206, pp. 451-454 (Larger Siṉṉamaṉūr plates).
9. *DCVP*, pp. 13-31.
10. *SCVP*, pp. 43-47.
11. *E.I.*, Vol. XXXVIII, No. 4, pp. 27-33.
12. *Ibid.*, p. 28.
13. K.V. Raman, *History of the Pāṇḍyas* (Tamil), Madras, 1977.
14. R. Nagaswamy, *TVCP.*
15. *E.I.*, Vol. XV, No. 5, pp. 58-66 (Anbil plates).

16. *E.I.*, Vol. XXII, No. 34, pp. 238-254 (Larger Leiden plates)
17. *S.I.I.*, Vol. III, No. 205, pp. 393-412 (Tiruvālaṅgāḍu plates.).
18. K.G. Krishnan, *KTPR*, pp. 69-193.
19. R. Nagaswamy, *ECPR*, pp. 31-51.
20. *E.I.*, Vol. XVIII, No. 4, pp. 31-48 (Kanyākumari inscription).
21. *E.I.*, Vol. IV, No. I, pp 4 -7 (Aihoḷe inscription)
22. D.B. Diskalkar, Dravidian and South Indian Inscriptions, *J.I.H.*, Vol. XXXIV, p. 173.

1

Pallava Inscriptions

The rule of the Pallava kings, which started from about the 4th century A.D. and continued till the ninth century A.D. was a glorious period in the literary history of the Tamil country. The Pallava rulers were very well-educated and some of these kings were great scholars as seen from their Sanskrit epigraphs.

Mahēndravarman I was the author of two Sanskrit plays *Mattavilāsaprahasana*[1] and *Bhagavadajjuka*.[2] He also made great contributions to the field of architecture and sculpture and to also the fine-arts like painting and music.

Some of the titles of Narasimhavarman II or Rājasiṁha such as *Śrī Itihāsa Priyaḥ* (one who is fond of Itihāsa) and *Śrī Kāvya Prabhōdhaḥ* (the reviver of poetry) found in one of his inscriptions[3] engraved in the Kailāsanātha temple at Kāñchīpuram the capital-city of the Pallava rulers, testify to his love of learning.

Again, in another inscription found in the Kandasvāmi temple at Tiruporūr in Chengalpattu district, he is called as *Jnāna Sāgara* (the ocean of knowledge).[4]

Similarly, Nandivarman II Pallavamalla was also a scholar and a poet. In the Kaśākuḍi copper-plate grant he is described as being like Brihaspati (the preceptor of gods) in knowledge (*tantrālāpavidhau svayam nayabharaḥ*) and that he was like Vālmīki in the composition of poetry (*kavitā-bandhē sa ādhyakaviḥ*).[5] Another inscription, the Udayēndiram copper-plates describe this king as being well-versed in poems, dramas and stories (*kāvya- nāṭakākhyāyikāsu pravīṇah*).[6] The same epigraph also states that he was skilled in metres such as Bindumati, Gūḍhachaturthapāda, Prahēḷika, Aksharachyutaka, and Mātrāchutaka.[7]

The kings of this dynasty honoured the scholars of their land and did their best to promote the cause of learning and literature. Sanskrit education in particular received special encouragement at the hands of these rulers. There were numerous educational institutions in the Pallava kingdom such as the *ghāṭika, śālai* and *vidyāsthāna* which sometimes functioned in the precincts of the temples, and also the *agrahāras* or the settlements of the brāhmaṇa scholars which were instrumental in the spread of the ancient brahmanical system of learning in which the texts were in Sanskrit. These centers of education received the personal attention of the rulers of the Pallava dynasty and their Sanskrit epigraphs speak of numerous endowments of money and land being made for the maintenance and promotion of these institutions.

The earliest Sanskrit inscriptions of Tamil Nadu were issued by the Pallava dynasty. As mentioned before, the early inscriptions of this dynasty have been discovered in several districts of Andhra Pradesh and of these, the Manchikallu,[8] Hirahadagalli[9] and Maidavolu[10] copper-plate charters were composed in Prakrit while the Gunapadeya[11] record is in Prakrit and Sanskrit. Subsequently, the other copper-plates of this dynasty, also found in the Andhra region like the Oṁgoḍu (I)[12] Uruvapaḷḷi,[13] Neḍungarāya,[14] Vēsanta,[15] Sakrēpaṭna,[16] Chēndalūr,[17] Omgōḍu (II),[18] Pikira,[19] Viḷāvaṭṭi[20] and Chura[21] copper-plate grants are fully in Sanskrit.

The earliest Sanskrit copper-plate grants discovered in Tamil Nadu are the Udayēndiram plates of Nandivarman I,[22] found at Udayēndiram (North Arcot district) belonging to c. 5th century A.D. and the Paḷḷankōvil copper-plate grant of Siṁhavarman found at Paḷḷankōvil (Thanjavur district) datable to c. 550 A.D.[23]

Later, in the period of Mahēndravarman I (600–630 A.D.), we come across many of his Sanskrit lithic inscriptions found on the walls of his cave temples at places like Dalavānūr (South Arcot district)[24], Mahēndravāḍi (North Arcot district)[25], Māmanḍūr (North Arcot district)[26] Maṇḍagapaṭṭu (South Arcot district)[27], Pallāvaram (Chengalpattu district)[28] and at Tiruchirāpaḷḷi.[29] His inscriptions which are of great importance to the world of South Indian music and which proclaim Mahēndravarman I to be a musical minded king are found at places like Kuḍimiyāmalai[30] and Tirummyam[31] (Pudukottai district). However, none of Mahēndravarman's epigraphs, except the one found at Tiruchirāpaḷḷi, can be stated to be of great literary merit.[32]

The Kūram copper-plate grant of the reign of Paramēśvaravarman I (670-691 A.D.) is a very important record from the view-point of literature as it is a *champu-kāvya* written partly in prose and partly in verse. Another inscription of the period of this ruler is found inscribed on the Gaṇeśa temple at Māmallapuram.[33] This record consisting of only eleven verses, is a lovely little poem describing Paramēśvaravarman's devotion to Lord Śiva. It states that he caused the shrine for Śiva (Dūrjaṭi) to be made. A duplicate of this same epigraph is found engraved in the Dharmarāja maṇḍapa at Māmallapuram.[34]

Subsequently, in the period of Rājasimha (691-728 A.D.), we do not find copper-plate grants discovered in Tamil Nadu, but some of his stone inscriptions are beautiful pieces of poetry. One of these is found in the Kailāśanātha temple in Kāñchīpuram and consists only of twelve verses and is a delectable poem.[35] Another of his records found in the Atiraṇachaṇḍēśvara temple, Śāluvankuppam (near Māmallapuram) and composed in seven stanzas is also a beautiful poem.[36]

It is in the reign of Nandivarman II Pallavamalla (731-796 A.D.), that numerous bi-lingual copper-plate grants were composed, the *praśasti* portions of which were written in beautiful Sanskrit prose and verse. These are the Udayēndiram plates (c. 752 A.D.),[37] the Kaśākuḍi plates (c. 753 A.D.),[38] the Pullūr plates (c. 764-65 A.D.),[39] the Tandantōṭṭam plates (c. 789 A.D.)[40] and the Paṭṭatāl-maṅgalam plates (c. 792 A.D.).[41]

Some of the other inscriptions which are of special importance as pieces of excellent poetry, belonging to the period of the later Pallavas are the Kumaraḍimaṅgalam[42] and Velūrpāḷayam plates (c. 852 A.D.)[43] of Nandivarman III (847-862 A.D.), the Chiṟṟūr plates (c. 875 A.D.)[44] and the Bāhūr plates (c. 877 A.D.)[45] of Nripatuṅgavarman and the Vēlāñjēri plates of Aparājita.[46]

These above-mentioned inscriptions have been taken up for a detailed study of the literary aspects in this chapter.

Poets of the Pallava Inscriptions

The Pallava kings patronized a number of poets and dramatists at their court. The famous Sanskrit poet, Bhāravi who wrote *Kirātarjunīyam* flourished in the court of Pallava Siṁhavishṇu.[47] Daṇḍin, who wrote the renowned Sanskrit works *Daśakumāracharita, Kavyādarsha and Avantisundarīkathā* was patronized by Pallava Rājasimha and lived in Kāñchīpuram. It is believed that Daṇḍin composed the *Kāvyādarsha* for giving lessons in rhetoric to a prince at Kāñchīpuram who was probably Rājasiṁha's son.[48] According to some scholars, it was probably Rājasiṁha himself who was Daṇḍin's pupil.[49]

Although the names of Bhāravi and Daṇḍin are famous till the present day due to their great works, there were a number of other talented scholars and poets who flourished in the Pallava kingdom and received encouragement from these kings. Although these poets must have composed many works, none of them have survived the passage of time and these outstanding literary giants can be known only through their inscriptional poems written about their royal patrons and inscribed for posterity on the walls of temples and on copper-plates which have withstood the test of time.

While the stone inscriptions unfortunately do not supply the names of these composers, luckily the copper-plate epigraphs almost always mention the name of the poets towards the concluding portions of these records.

The very first copper-plate inscription which mentions the name of the poet-composer of the Sanskrit *praśasti* is the Paḷḷankōvil record of Pallava Simhavarman, datable to c.550 A.D. The author of this record was a scholar named Mēdhāvi, who is described in this inscription as 'one who was proficient in ṭhe *śāstras*, respectable, and was like Brihaspati in intelligence'.

समस्तशास्त्रनिष्णातः धिषणो धिषणोपमः ।
मान्यो नाम्नापि मेधावि प्रशस्तिं कृतवान् इमाम् ।।

(samasta-śāstra-nishṇātah dhishaṇō dhishaṇōpamaḥ,
mānyō nāmnāpi Mēdhāvi praśastim kṛitavān imām)[50]

Another copper-plate grant which supplies the name of the poet who wrote the verses of the Sanskrit *praśasti* portion is the Kaśākuḍi copper-plate epigraph (c. 753-59 A.D.) of the reign of Nandivarman II Pallavamalla. This composer's name was Trivikrama and a verse at the end of the Sanskrit section describes him as 'one who was honest, who knew the truth of all sciences and performed sacrifices according to the rules of the three Vēdas'.

अकृत्रिमस्त्रयी विधिक्रमक्रतु प्रवर्तकः।
समस्तशास्त्रतत्ववित् प्रशस्तिकृत् त्रिविक्रमः।।

(akritimastrayī vidhi krama-kratu-pravartakaḥ samastaśāstra tatvavit praśastikṛit Trivikramaḥ)[51]

One more copper-plate epigraph of the period of Nandivarman II Pallavamalla, the Udayēndiram plates (c. 752 A.D.) states that the poet of this charter was Paramēśvara, who was the son of Chandradēva and who belonged to the race of Mēdhāvi.

पुत्रः श्रीचन्द्रदेवस्य कविस्तु परमेश्वरः।
प्रशस्तेः कविताञ्चक्रे स मेधाविकुलोद्भवः।।

(putraḥ Śrīchandradēvasya kavistu Paramēśvaraḥ praśastēḥ kavitāñchakrē sa Mēdhāvi-kulōdbhavaḥ)[52]

The Sanskrit section of the Taṇḍantōṭṭam plates (c. 789 A.D.) was also composed during the reign of the same king by a poet named Paramēśvara, surnamed Uttarakāraṇika, the son of Paramōttarakāraṇika, 'the self-chosen lord of poetry'.

परमोत्तरकारणिकस्याकृत कविता स्वयंवृतवरस्य।
उत्तरकारणिकाख्यस्तनयः परमेश्वरः पशस्तिमिमाम्।।

(Paramōttarakāraṇikasyākṛita kavitā-svayamvṛita-varasya Uttarakāraṇikākhyastanayaḥ Paramēśvaraḥ praśastim imām)[53]

It is possible that since both the Udayēndiram and the Taṇḍantōṭṭam plates were composed during the reign of Nandivarman II Pallavamalla, and since the time gap between the two compositions was only seven years, the poet Paramēśvara who composed the *praśasti* section of the Udayēndiram charter could be the very same Paramēśvara, surnamed Uttarakāraṇika, of the Taṇḍantōṭṭam plates, and Chandradẹva, the poet's father (mentioned in the Udayēndiram plates) could be the same as Paramōttarakāraṇika (of the Tandantōṭṭam plates).[54]

As the Udayēndiram plates state that poet Paramēśvara was born in the family of Mēdhāvi, it is possible that the latter was the composer of the Paḷḷankōvil grant mentioned earlier.[55]

According to the Vēlūrpāḷayam copper-plate grant (c. 852 A.D.) of the reign of Nandivarman III, the poet of the Sanskrit *praśasti* of this charter was Mahēśvara Manōdhīra.

वाग्मनःकायकर्म्माणि परार्थान्येव यस्य सः।
महेश्वरो मनोधीरः पशस्तिं कृतवानिमाम्।।

(vāgmanaḥ-kāyakarmmāṇi parārtthānyēva yasya saḥ
Mahēśvaro Manōdhīraḥ praśastim kṛitavānimām)[56]

The Bāhūr copper-plate inscription (c. 877 A.D.) of the period of Nṛipatuṅgavarman, which speaks of the existence of an educational center (*vidyāsthāna*) at Bāhūr (present-day Vāgur near Pondicherry) mentions that the poet who composed the Sanskrit section of this charter was Nāgaya, a pious person and who was a servant of the seat of learning of the residents of the village of Bāhūr.

दासस्स्थानस्य विद्यायाः बाहुर्ग्रामजुषामयं।
कृतवान् शास्त्रतत्त्वज्ञः प्रशस्तिन्दासयस्स्वतः।।

Dāsas-sthānasya vidhyāyāḥ bāhūr-grāmajushāmayam
Kṛitavān śāstra-tattvajñaḥ praśastin-dāsayassvataḥ.[57]

The Chiṟṟūr plates (c. 875 A.D.) of the same king mention a poet named Kumāra as the composer of the Sanskrit verses. He is described as a highly intelligent person, of praiseworthy conduct and very knowledgeable:

कृतवा नाकृतकहृदः कृती कृतज्ञः कविः।
कुमाराख्यः विद्यानद्युम्बुनिधिः प्रशस्तशीलः प्रशस्तिमिमाम्।।

(kṛitavā nākṛitaka-hṛidaḥ kṛitī kṛitajnaḥ kavih
Kumārākhyaḥ vidhyā-nadyambu-nidhiḥ prasasta-sīlaḥ
praśastim imām)[58]

The latest copper-plate grant discovered so far of the Pallava period, the Vēḷāñjēri plates, belonging to the reign of Aparājita states that it was composed by Mahādēva, the son of Śrī Kumāra who was the composer of *mahākāvyas* and who set aside the eloquence of his rivals.

विपक्षवादि प्रतिभावहर्तुः कर्तुं र्महाकाव्यनिबन्धनानां।
कृतामहादेव-समाह्वयेन प्रशस्तिरेषा तनयेन तस्य।।

(vipakshavādi pratibhāva-hartuḥ kartur mahākāvya-nibhandanānām
kṛitā Mahādēva samāhvayēna praśastirēsha tanayēna tasya)[59]

The Chiṟṟūr plates mentioned earlier were composed by Kumāra and the Vēḷāñjēri record was composed by poet Mahādēva, son of Śrī Kumāra. It is possible that since these two records were composed during the reigns of Nṛipatuṅgavarman and Aparājita respectively, Kumāra of the Chiṟṟūr record could have been the father of Mahādēva both father and son serving at the royal court.[60]

It is rather unfortunate that a few of the copper-plate inscriptions like the Kūram plates of Paramēśvaravarman and the Pūllur and Paṭṭātalmaṅgalam plates of Nandivarman II Pallavamalla as well as the stone inscriptions of the Pallava period do not mention the names of the talented people who composed these beautiful poems.

Literary Beauty of the Pallava Inscriptions

The Sanskrit inscriptions of the Pallavas, especially the copper-plate grants, contain many verses as well as prose passages which are of great literary merit. In the following pages an attempt has been made to highlight some of these portions which are written in elegant language and reveal the skill and imagination of the poets who composed them.

The Paḷḷankōvil inscription of Siṁhavarman contains a beautiful verse, which describes the qualities of this king and also gives a picturesque, vivid description of the Chōḷa land:

'He in whom the group of virtues (beginning with) truthfulness, sacrifice and modesty had found an abode and in whom the quality of warriors had become very highly developed (to the extent) not found in anyone else, conquered the land of the Chōḷas which had as its garland the daughter of Kavēra (i.e. the river Kāvērī) and as its waistband, the rice-fields, rich fields of sugarcane, the groves of palm-trees, plantains and the like'.

सत्यत्यागविनीततादि विमलं यस्मिन्नलब्धास्पदं।
वृन्दं क्षात्रगुणं समुन्नतमताऽन्येष्वलब्धास्पदं।।
येना हारितरां कवेरतनया हारापि चोलावनिश्शाले।
येक्षु वनांशुक क्रमुकरम्भारामसन् मेखला।।

(satya- tyāga- vinītatādivimalam yasminn-labdāspadam
vṛindam kshātraguṇam sammunatamatā-anyēshu-alabdāspadam
yēnāhāritarām kavēratanayā-hārāpi Chōḷāvaniś-śāle-
yēkshu-vanāmśuka-kramuka-rambārāmasan mēkhalā)[61]

An epigraph of Mahēndravarman I is found on the upper rock-cut cave temple at Tiruchirāpaḷḷi[62] in two parts, engraved on two pilasters flanking a large panel of the story of Lord Śiva receiving the river Gaṅgā on his matted hair (Gaṅgādhara). This epigraph consisting totally of eight verses in various metres like *śārdūlavikṛīditā, āryā, anusṭubh* and vasantatilakā and couched in beautiful language mentions that this king built this wonderful stone-temple for Śiva and adds very poetically that:

'Being afraid that the God who is fond of rivers (*nadipriyaḥ*), i.e., Śiva, having perceived Kāvērī, whose waters please the eye, who wears a garland of gardens and who possesses lovely qualities might fall in love with her, the daughter of the mountain, Pārvatī, has I think left her father's family and resides permanently on this mountain, calling this river the beloved of the Pallava king.'

कावीरीन्नयनाभिराम सलिलामाराममालाधराम्।
देवो वीक्ष्य नदीप्रियः प्रियगुणामप्येष रज्येदिति।।

सा शंका गिरिकन्यका पितृकुलं हित्वेह मन्ये गिरौ।
नित्यन्तिष्ठति पल्लवस्य दयितामेतां ब्रुवाणा नदीम्।।

(*Kāvirīnnayanā-bhirāma-salilām ārāma-māladharām,*
dēvō vīkshya nadīpriyaḥ priyaguṇāmāpyēsha rajyēditi,
saśamkhā giri-kanyakā pitrikulam hitvēha manyē girau
nityantiśṭhati Pallavasya dayitām yētām bruvāṇā nadīm).

According to some scholars, this poetic inscription was the composition of king Mahēndravarman I himself and that the eight-verse text of the inscription is as remarkable a piece of adoration of Nadipriya, evidently meaning here Gaṅgādhara, as the masterly panel of Gaṅgādhara on either side of which the epigraph is engraved.[63]

In the period of Mahēndravarman's successor, Narasiṁhavarman I (630-668 A.D.) and Mahēndravarman II (668-670 A.D.), we do not come across any Sanskrit epigraphs of exceptional literary merit, but during the reign of Paramēśvaravarman I (670-691 A.D.), we find the famous Kūram copper-plate grant of this ruler[64] found at the village of Kūram, near Kāñchīpuram, the Pallava capital city. This bi-lingual record, the first portion of which is in Sanskrit and the latter half in Tamil, gives a graphic description of the battle of Peruvaḻanallūr fought between the Pallava and Chāḷukyan armies.

This record abounds in *ślēsha*. An example of *sabhaṅga ślēsha* is seen in line 18 of this record, which describes the son of Mahēndravarman (Paramēśvaravarman) as 'one by whom prosperity was thoroughly produced (*su-rachita*), just as prosperity is heaped on the Gods (*sura-chita*)', by Mahēndra.

महेन्द्रस्येव सुरचित संपदो महेन्द्रवर्म्मणः।।

Examples of *abhaṅga ślēsha* are seen in the next few lines 19, 20 and 21, in which Paramēśvaravarman is described as 'conqueror of all' (*sarvadamana*) and thus compared to

Bharata (son of Śakūntalā and Dushyanta, also called Sarvadamana); as one who avoided all improper conduct (*asamañja*), just as Sagara abandoned his son Asamañja; and who possessed a strong body (*aṅga*), just as Karṇa was the king of Aṅga

भरत इव सर्वदमनः, सगर इव कृतासमञ्जस त्यागः,
कर्ण इव पुष्कलाङ्गः।

(Bharata iva sarvadamanaḥ, sagara iva kṛitāsamañjasa tyagaḥ Karṇa iva pushkalāngaḥ)

The poet then describes in a very long prose passage, the marching of the Pallava army, and the fight itself and compares this with unseasonal rains (*vikāla varshāvatāra iva*), in which the swinging of the unsheathed swords appeared like the flashes of lightening (*vikōśa nistrimśa vidyudābhōgē*) and the movement of the army elephants was like thunder-clouds (*pracharita kuñjara jaladē*).

The composer then very poetically describes this hard-fought war, in which both sides sometimes gained and lost as follows: 'the Goddess of Fortune was sitting on the swing of doubt about mutual victory or defeat'

अन्योन्य जयपराजय सन्देह प्रेङ्खलग्न लक्ष्मी विहिते।

(anyōnya jaya-parājaya sandēha prēnkha-lagna Lakshmī vihite)

Another epigraph of Paramēśvaravarman I found in the rock-cut Gaṇēśa temple[65] and also in the Dharmarāja-maṇḍapa[66] at Māmallapuram, the sea-port town of the Pallavas, consisting of eleven verses in the *āryā* and *anushṭubh* metres in very simple, but chaste Sanskrit describes this king's devotion to Śiva, called in these few verses by many of his names like Śaṁbhu, Bhava, Sthānu, Śaṅkara, Dhūrjaṭi, Kāmamardana and Hara and records that he caused these temples for Śiva to be made.

There are a large number of stone inscriptions of Paramēśvaravarman's son and successor, Narasiṁhavarman

II also known as Rājasiṁha (691-728 A.D.) found inscribed on the structural temples which he built such as the Shore temple at Māmallapuram,[67] the Kailāsanātha temple at Kāñchīpuram[68] and the Tāḷagīriśvara temple at Panamalai[69] (South Arcot district). These lithic inscriptions are mostly very short and contain many of his titles (*birudas*) and extol his devotion to Śiva. Of these, one particular record, found outside the central shrine of the Kailāsanātha temple, written in the ornate Pallava-Grantha script, so characteristic of that period, in twelve verses in a single line, deserves special mention. This lithic inscriptional poem begins with an invocation to the sacred river Gaṅgā.

The versatile unnamed poet of this record using his vivid imagination speaks of the Gaṅgā, which descends from the head of Sthānu (Śiva), the sparkling gem (*Sthanu-ratnāt*) and fills up the deep lake of the universe, which is the ocean (*tribhuvana-saras*). As the Gaṅgā begins her descent from Śiva's head, her waters assume different colours like white, black, blue, red and again blue, reflecting the colours by coming into contact respectively with the white rays of the moon, adorning Śiva's head; with the dark matted locks on His head below the moon; with the blue poison in his neck; with the red rays of the gems of the snakes worn by Śiva (as *nāgābharaṇa*); and with the rays of the gems of the ornaments of Pārvatī nearby (who is believed to be blue-complexioned).[70]

The Pallava rulers seemed to have had a fascination for the Gaṅgāvataraṇa or 'descent of the Gaṅgā' theme as seen from Mahēndravarman's poem etched in Tiruchirāpaḷḷi mentioned earlier; the world-famous bas-relief sculpture of the same theme (renowned as Bhagīratha's penance) at Māmallapuram of the reign of Narasimhavarman I and found again in this tiny poem on the walls of the Kailāsanātha temple.[71]

The poet, after giving the mythical genealogy of the Pallava-vaṁśa and the predecessors of Rājasiṁha, very poetically describes this king as being like Manmatha (the God of love) in the art of pleasing women well-versed in the different arts in private; Indra in protecting those who follow the path of the Vēdas; Vishṇu in breaking the hearts of the foes of the sages, the twice-born and the Gods; and Kubēra in pleasing the virtuous by means of riches. Thus, in this verse, the poet refers to *kāma, dharma, mōksha* and *artha,* 'the four *purushārthas* of Hindu tradition and show how intelligently this king enjoyed and supported them appropriately.[72]

During the period of Nandivarman II Pallavamalla (731-796 A.D.), a large number of bi-lingual copper-plate grants were issued by this king such as the Udayēndiram, Kaśākuḍi, Pullūr, Taṇḍantōttam and the Paṭṭaṭālmaṅgalam inscriptions. These charters contain Sanskrit *praśasti* portions, composed in verse and sometimes in prose.

The first of these, the Udayēndiram plates (c. 752 A.D.), contains only eight verses, but in five different metres, and the rest of the *praśasti* portion is in prose, thus revealing this inscription to be a beautiful *champu kāvya.* The poet of this *praśasti,* named Paramēśvara, who has employed a large number of *alaṅkāras* to embellish and beautify this record, in two particular prose passages has used the *mālōpama alaṅkāra* to describe his patron and king and in between these two passages has inserted a *luptōpama alaṅkāra* and this in total has a very beautifying effect overall thus:

भरत इव सर्वदमनः, मेरुरिव अचलः
दिवसकरइव स्वकरैरेव रिपुतमस निरोध भेदकः,
शशधर इव सकलकलापरिणतः

Bharata iva Sarvadamanaḥ Mērur iva achlaḥ
divasakara iva svakarair eva, ripu tamasa nirōda bhēdakaḥ,
śaśadhara iva sakalakalāpariṇataḥ

Followed by *luptōpama:*

दिगन्त विजृम्भमाण कुमुदवनविपुलकीर्त्तिः

Diganta vijrimbamāṇa kumudavanavipulakīrtiḥ

And again *malōpama:*

कुसुमचाप इव वपुषि, वत्सराज इव कुञ्जरेषु।
नकुल इव तुरङ्गमेषु, अर्जुन इव कार्मुके, द्रोण इव धनुर्वेदे।।

Kusuma-chāpa iva vapushi, vatsarāja iva kuñjarēshu, nakula iva turaṅgamēshu, Arjuna iva kārmukē Drōṇa iva dhanurvēdē.[73]

In verse four, which is in *jagati-indravamśa* metre, following the above mentioned prose passage, the king is described as being different to different people.

'The virtuous Nandivarma, the lord of the Pallavas, was like death to his enemies, Cupid to women, unconquerable by armies, rich in virtues, the refuge of his subjects and *kalpa* tree to good men'.

कृतान्तोरिपूणां अनङ्गो वधूनां।
अलङ्घ्योबलानां अनूनोगुणानां।।
शरण्यः प्रजानां सतां कल्पवृक्षः।
कृती नन्दिवर्मा पतिः पल्लवानाम्।।

(kritāntō ripūṇām anangō vadhūnām
alangyō balānām anuno guṇānām
śaraṇyaḥ prajānām satām kalpavrikshaḥ
kritī Nandivarma patiḥ Pallavānām)[74]

In the Kaśākuḍi plates of the same ruler, which is also a *champu kāvya,* the poet Trivikrama uses the *upamā dhvani* in a couple of verses. In verse nine of this record which is in *indravajra* metre, he refers without mentioning the name itself, to the king Nandivarman II whose father was Hiraṇya and the epithets which this king receives in the first half of the verse are at the same time surnames of Brahmā, Vishṇu and Śiva and thus hints at a comparison of the king to each of these three gods.

हिरण्यगर्भो जयति प्रजापतिः
श्रियःपतिश्शाक्करकेतनः क्षितिम्
सहेल कल्लोल समुद्रवारणां
बलद्विषा यस्य सपत्न वारणाः।।

(Hiraṇya-garbho jayati prajāpatiḥ
śrīyaḥ patis śākvara-kētanaḥ kshitim
sahēla kallōla samudra vāraṇām
bala-dvishā yasya sapatna vāraṇaḥ)[75]

In verse twenty-four in *vasantatilakā* metre, the poet again employs the *upamā dhvani*. The comparison with Śiva is based on the name of Paramēśvara (Nandivarman II), which is at the same time one of the names of Śiva.

'This wonderful king possessed high prosperity (*bhūti*) was the lord of men (*bhūta*), had a bull for his crest and a club on his banner and possessed immovable firmness (thus resembling Śiva who wears sacred ashes (*bhūti*) is the lord of the goblins (*bhūta*), has a bull for his emblem and a club on his banner and resides on a mountain'.

इच्छा विधेय सकलावनिपाललोकः।
पश्चादबभूव परमेश्वरपोतवर्मा।।
भूतिं परां वहति भूतपतिर्वृषाङ्कः।
खट्वाङ्गकेतुरचल स्थितिरद्भुतो यः।।

(iccha vidhēya sakala avanipāla lōkaḥ
paschād babhūva Paramēśvarapōtavarmā
bhūtim parām vahati bhūtapatir vrishānkaḥ
khatvāṅga-kēturachala-sthitiradbuto yaḥ)[76]

In a prose passage in this inscription, the composer employs *ślēsha alaṅkāra* while describing the Pallava kings in general, using the technical points of grammar to bring out a very simple idea, but expressed very beautifully thus:

'They (the Pallava kings) experienced an increase (*āgama*) of the affection (*pratyaya*) of their subjects (*prakriti*) and possessed faultless riches (*vṛiddhi*) and virtues (*guṇas*) and therefore resembled the science of grammar in which the crude form (*prakriti*) affixes (*pratyaya*) and augments (*āgamas*) are treated, but in which the rules on *guṇa* and *vṛiddhi* are not without exceptions'.[77]

शब्दागम इव प्रकृतिप्रत्ययागमोपेता निरपवाद वृद्धिगुणाश्च

(śabdāgama iva prakṛti pratyayāgamōpēta nirapavāda vṛiddhi guṇascha).

Similarly, the composer of this charter in a prose passage speaks of the Pallava race which had descended from Aśōkavarman in a verse with alliteration:

'From him descended the powerful, spotless race of Pallavas which resembled a partial incarnation of Vishṇu, as it displayed unbroken courage in conquering the circle of the world with all its parts, and as it enforced the rules of all castes and orders and which resembled the descent of the Gaṅgā on earth as it purified the whole world'.

ततः प्रभृत्यखण्ड कलभुवनमण्डलात्मसात्करणा खण्डितविक्रमपर परिपालित सकल वर्णाश्रम व्यवस्था विशेषः प्रभविष्णुः विष्णोः अंशावतार इव वंशावतारः पल्लवानां अखिलभुवन पावनतया गंगावतार इव च निर्मल समवर्तत।

(tataḥ prabhriti akhaṇḍa-kala-bhuvana-maṇḍalāt karaṇākhaṇḍita vikrama paraḥ paripālita sakala varṇāśrama vyavastha visēshaḥ prabha Vishnuḥ Vishnōḥ amśāvatāra iva vamśāvatāraḥ Pallavānām akhila bhuvana pāvanataya Gaṅgāvatāra iva cha nirmala samavarttata.)[78]

In the same inscription, in the prose section, the donee, a brāhmaṇa scholar named Jyeshṭhapāda Sōmayājin who received a land-grant from Nandivarman II Pallavamalla is very poetically described by seven epithets, which begin successively with the numbers one to seven. He is stated to be a unique person, who cares for both worlds (for earthly as well as heavenly prosperity), who accomplishes the three objects of human life (*trivarga*), who knows the four Vēdas, whose chief objects are the five primary elements (*pañchamahābhūta*), who knows the six auxiliary works and who resembles the sun.

एक पुरुषाय, द्विलोकचिन्तनाय, त्रिवर्गसाधकाय, चतुर्वेदाय पञ्चमहाभूतपरार्थाय, षडंगाय, सप्तसप्तिप्रतिमाय।

(*ēka purushāya dvilōkachintanāya trivarga-sādakāya chaturvēdāya pañcha-mahābhūta-parārtāya shaḍaṅgāya sapta sapti pratimāya.*)[79]

In the Taṇḍantoṭṭam plates we come across a verse in praise of the king where the poet uses the pronoun *yad śabdha* in all seven cases:

यस्सच्चक्रस्य भर्ता हरिरिव विबुधाश्शक्रवद्यं श्रयन्ते
येनाभूद्भूस्सनाथा सुचरितनममलं रोचते चारु यस्मै
यस्माद्भीरेकधीराद्युधि परनृभुजां यस्य कीर्त्यादशाशाः
संपूर्णाः, श्रीश्च यस्मिन्निवसति सुचिरन्त्यक्त चापल्य दोषा।

Yussuchchakrasyabharta harıriva vibudhāśśakravadyam śrayante
Yēnābhūd bhū-ssanāthā sucharitamamalam rōchate charu yasmai
Yasmādbhīrēka dhīrādyudhi para nṛibhujām yasya kīrtyā daśāśāḥ
Sampurṇāḥ śrīscha yasmin nivasati suchiran tyakta-chāpalya dōśhā.[80]

He is the lord of the circle of good people, as Hari is the possessor of the powerful weapon *chakra*. Him the wise cling to as gods to Śakra (Indra). By him the earth has become coupled with a husband. To whom faultless good deeds are most welcome. At whom –the sole hero- on the battle-field the enemy kings take fright. The fame of whom fills the ten quarters, and in whom Śrī (Lakshmī), dwells permanently abandoning her vice of fickleness.

Invocatory Verses

The Sanskrit inscriptions of the Pallava period, especially

the copper-plate grants, usually commence with a few verses in praise of various Gods and Goddesses of the Hindu pantheon like Vishṇu, Śiva, Lakshmī, Pārvatī and Gaṇēśa. Some of these verses are full of poetic beauty and reveal the power of imagination of the poet-composers of these charters.

The Pallava rulers were eclectic in their religious outlook. Whatever be the personal faith of a ruler, he never prevented his royal poets from composing verses to deities of their choice. Nandivarman II Pallavamalla, for example was a great devotee of Vishṇu and poetically proclaims in the Taṇḍantōṭṭam copper-plates that 'his head never knew of bowing down to others except to the pair of worshipful feet of Mukunda'.

मूर्धन्यत्र मुकुन्दवन्द्यचरणद्वन्द्वं विहायापरेष्वज्ञातप्रणतः

(mūrdhanyatra Mukunda-vandhya-charaṇa-dvandvam vihāyāparēshvagñāta praṇataḥ).[81]

Yet, his inscriptions such as the Kaśākuḍi and Udayēndiram records contain stanzas in praise of Śiva. In fact, the Udayēndiram plates open with a stanza about Śiva and this record does not contain any verse on Vishṇu.

Generally, Sanskrit texts begin in three different ways namely *āśi* (benediction), *namaskriya* (salutations) and *vastu-nirdēśa* (start the topic directly). All the three types are found in these Sanskrit epigraphs. Examples of the *āśi* type are found in almost all the copper-plate inscriptions; an example of *namaskriya* is found in the Udayēndiram record and *vastu-nirdēśa* in the Tandantōṭṭam plates.

Vishṇu

The Pallava Sanskrit epigraphs contain a number of invocatory verses in praise of Vishṇu, mentioned by many of his names and epithets like Achyuta, Hari, Janārdana, Jishṇu, Mādhava, Madhusūdana, Mukunda, Narakāri, Pankajanābha and Trivikrama.

Some very beautiful stanzas about this deity can be found in the Kaśākuḍi,[82] Paṭṭatālmaṅgalam,[83] Bāhūr[84] and Vēḷāñjēri[85] copper-plate grants.

In the second verse of the Kāśakuḍi plates, the composer invokes the blessings of Lord Vishṇu in his incarnation (*avatāra*) as Trivikrama thus:

'May that blessed Trivikrama (Vishṇu) grant you prosperity, who, at the sacrifice of Bali deceitfully asked (only) for three steps (of land) but suddenly strode thrice (thereby) appropriating the worlds'.

मायाविना येन पदत्रयार्त्थिना सद्यः
प्रवृद्धेन पुनर्बलेर्मखे
विचक्रमे त्रिजगतस्स्वसात्कृतौ स वः
अस्तु भूत्यै भगवान्स्त्रिविक्रमः

(mayāvīna yēna padatrayā-rtthinā sadyaḥ
pravriddhēna punarbalērmakhē
vichakramē trijagatas svasātkritau sa vaḥ
astu bhūtyai Bhagavānstrivikramaḥ)

The Paṭṭatālmaṅgalam plates state in the very first verse of this inscription:

'May that body of the husband of Śrī (i.e. Vishṇu) which is resplendent with the kaustubha jewel on its chest and which, with marakata-like arms is lying on the ocean, resembling a collection of clouds lustrous, with the interspersed lightning and settling on the waters of the ocean to imbibe (its) water, grant you welfare'.

श्रियो भर्तुर्मूर्ति र्मरकतसमानै र्भुजशतै
श्शयानस्याम्भोधावुरसि विलसत् कौस्तुभरुचिः
पयः पातुं सिन्धोर्ज्जलधरघटेवाप्सु पतिता
तटिद्युक्ता भान्ति दिशतु भवताम्मङ्गलमसौ

(Śryīo bhartur mūrttir marakata-samānair bhujaśatais
śayānasyāmbhōdhāvurasi vilasat koustubha-ruchiḥ

payaḥ pātum sindhōr jaladhara-gaṭevāpsu patitā
taṭityuktha bhānti diśatu bhavatām maṅgaḷam asau.)

Another beautiful invocatory verse about Vishṇu in the *drutavilambita* metre is found in the Bāhūr copper-plate grant of Nṛipatuṅgavarman. Here, the poet of this charter named Nāgaya speaks of Vishṇu thus:

'Let Madhu's destroyer (Vishṇu) grant you prosperity, the lotus-eyed one, whose feet are rubbed by the diadems of the Gods (bowing to him), the unborn one (who became) the means of the destruction of demons that terrified the whole world.'

श्रियमम्बुजलोचन स्त्रिदशमौलि निसृष्टपदाम्बुजः
सकललोक भयंकरराक्षसप्रशमहेतु रजो मधुसूदन

(Śriam aṁbuja-lōchana-stridaśa-mouḷi-nisrishṭa-padāmbujaḥ sakala-lōka bhayaṅkara-rākshasa-praśama-hētu-rajaḥ Madhusūdanaḥ)

And lastly, the Vēḷāñjēri copper-plate grant of Aparājita, one of the very last bi-lingual grants of the Pallava dynasty discovered till now, contains yet another poetic description of this God which runs as follows:

'Let Janārdana, who is ever united with Śrī, who wields the resplendent conch and discus, wears a coral garland, dark in colour like the one which came forth when the Gods and demons churned the ocean, and who entered another ocean to protect us.'

लक्ष्मीश्रितानिमिषमुज्वलशङ्खचक्रं
प्रच्छाय विद्रुमलताधरमञ्जनाभं
सिन्धोः सुरासुर विनिर्मथितादिवान्यं
सिन्धुं ययौ यमवतात् सजनार्दनो वः

(Lakshmī sritānimishāmudjvala śanka-chakram
prachchāya viddruma-latādharamajjanābham
sindhōḥ surāsura vinirmatitādivānyam
sindhum yayau yam avatāt sa Janārdhanō vaḥ)

Śiva

There are a very large number of invocatory verses praising Śiva in the lithic and copper-plate grants of the Pallava dynasty. He is mentioned by many of his names and epithets like Chandramouḷi, Bhavānīpati, Dhūrjaṭi, Hara, Indumouḷi, Paramēśvara, Pinākapāṇi, Śaśānkamouḷi, Śrīkaṇṭa, Śaṅkara, Śaṁbu, Śarva, Triśūli, and Purahara.

One of the earliest lithic records of the Pallava period which contains an invocatory verse in *virōdhābhāsa alaṅkāra* about Śiva, inscribed during the period of Paramēśvaravarman I in the Gaṇēśa temple[86] and the Dharmarāja Maṇḍapa at Māmallapuram[87] by an unknown poet reads:

'May (Śiva) the destroyer of love, who is the cause of production, existence and destruction, (but himself) without cause, fulfill the boundless desires of men'.

संभवस्थितिसंहारकारणं वीतकारणः ।
भूयात् अत्यन्त कामाय जगतां काममर्द्धनः ।।

(saṁbhava-sthiti-samhāra-kāraṇam vītakāraṇaḥ
bhūyāt atyantakāmāya jagatām kāmamarddanaḥ)

Among the copper-plates grants which open with stanzas praising Śiva are Kūram,[88] Udayēndiram,[89] Kaśākuḍi,[90] Vēlūrpāḷayam[91] and Vēḷāñjēri[92] plates of Aparājita.

Among these, the invocatory verses found in the Kaśākuḍi plates composed in the *śārdūlavikrīḍita* metre gives a complete description of this deity as he has been represented in the epics and Purāṇas as follows:

'May Hara (Śiva) the destroyer of Pura, increase your happiness, who bears the moon on his crest, who wears a serpent on his shoulder, who holds Bhavānī on his left, who bears affection to his worshipper, who bears Gaṅgā on his head, who wears ashes on his body, who bears poison in his neck, who wears a braid in his hair and who holds a spear in his hand'.

मौलाविन्दुधरः फणाधरधरः स्कन्धे भवानीधरो
वामे, कामधरः प्रणामनिरते, गंगाधरो मूर्धनि।
मूर्त्तौ धूलीधरो गळे गरधरः केशेषु वेणीधरः
पाणौ शूलधरो हरः पुरहरः पुष्णातु वो मङ्गलम्।।

(maulavindudharaḥ phaṇādharadharaḥ skandē Bhavānīdharō vāmē kāmadharaḥ praṇāmaniratē Gaṅgādharō mūrdhani murtau dhūḷidharō gaḷē garadharaḥ kēśēshu vēṇīdharaḥ pāṇau śūladharo Haraḥ puraharaḥ pushṇātu vō maṅgalam)

A similar lengthy beautiful verse in *śragdhara* metre in the Kūram charter invokes the protection of Śiva who has five faces, fifteen fearful eyes, bears the moon on his crest, who bears the trident, whose sacred thread is a terrible serpent, who possesses ten strong arms, who has the form of the universal soul which consists of truth alone, the divine one, who is to be respected by Mukunda and gods, who produces the creation, who is propitiated by spells, the creator, who is knowledge incarnate, who exercises self-restraint and whose form is the universe.

पञ्चास्यस्त्रिंशदर्द्धः प्रतिभयनयनः चन्द्रमौळिस्त्रिशूली
भीमव्यालोपवीती दशभुजपरिघस्तत्वमात्रात्म मूर्त्तिः।
दिव्योवेक्ष्यो मुकुन्दप्रभृतिभिरमरैस्सृष्टिकृन्मन्त्रसिद्धः
कर्ता नो मूर्तविद्या विहितपरयमस्त्रायतां विश्वमूर्तिः।।

*(panchāsyas-trimśadardhaḥ prati-bhaya nayanas chandra-mouḷistriśūli
bhīma-vyalōpa-vīti daśabhujaparighas tatva-mātrātma-mūrtiḥ
divyōvēkshyō Mukundaprabhritibhiramaraisrishtikrit-mantra-siddhaḥ
karta nō mūrta-vidyā vihitaparayamastrāyatām viśva-mūrtiḥ)*

Gaṇēśa

It is normally a custom in India, starting from the ancient period, to begin any work only after paying obeisance to Lord Gaṇēśa, the remover of all obstacles. However, a study of the Sanskrit inscriptions of the Pallavas reveals that only one record, namely the Kaśākuḍi plates[93] contains an invocation to this deity.

It is generally believed that the cult of Gaṇēśa became extremely popular to the Tamil country after the conquest of Vātāpi (modern Badami in Karnataka), the capital-city of the Western Chālukyas by Narasimhavarman I in the 7th century A.D. from where an idol of Gaṇēśa was brought to the ancient Tamil country.[94]

It is therefore not surprising to notice the absence of verses on this deity before the period of this inscription dated c. 753-54 A.D. as the cult of Gaṇēśa may not have been very widespread in the Pallava kingdom. It is very surprising to note that none of the other inscriptions composed after the Kaśākuḍi plates contain any invocatory verses or even references to this deity.

It would however not be out of place to mention the description of Gaṇēśa as painted in poetic language by Trivikrama, the poet of the Kaśākuḍi grant, as it describes this God with the very same characteristics as he is found described in many of the Purāṇas and other religious literature of ancient India.

'May Vināyaka (Gaṇēśa) grant you freedom from obstacles, who is white as the Kailāśa (mountain) whose girdle consists of a huge serpent, who has the face of an elephant , whose ears are large, who has a single big tusk, and whose eyes are (half closed as if he were) under the influence of rut'.

कैलासगौरः पृथु नाग कक्ष्यः
प्रोद्वृत्तकर्णो बृहदेकदन्तः।
मातङ्गवक्त्रो मदनिग्ननेत्रो
भूयादविघ्नाय विनायको वः।।

(Kailāsagauraḥ pṛithu-nāga-kakshyaḥ
prōddvṛitta karṇō bṛihadēkadantaḥ
mātaṅga-vaktrō mada-nignanētrō
bhūyādavighnāya Vināyakō vaḥ)

Apart from the invocatory verses about Vishṇu, Śiva, and Gaṇēśa, there are also some stanzas which invoke the blessings of the Supreme Being or Creator without naming him specifically.

The Kaśākuḍi plates record 'Victorious is the supreme Brahman, which is the cause of the production, stability, and destruction of the three worlds, which is true without end (and) without beginning, which consists of knowledge alone, which is one (and) which is the abode of immortality'.

जयति जगत्त्रयजन्मस्थितिसंहृतिकारणं परब्रह्म।
सत्यमनन्तमनादि ज्ञानात्मकमेकममृतपदम्।।

(jayati jagattraya janma-sthiti-samhriti kāraṇm parabrahma
satyam-anantam- anādi jnanātmakam ēkam amṛita-padam.)[95]

Similar verses are also found in the Velūrpāḷayam[96] and the Paṭṭatālmaṅgalam[97] plates.

Lakshmī

In comparison with the invocatory stanzas about Gods, the ones in praise of Goddesses are much less in number. Only one Pallava epigraph, the Kaśākuḍi grant[98] contains a verse invoking the blessings of Lakshmī, the consort of Vishṇu, thus:

'May Padmā (Lakshmī) regard you with fondness, who is seated on a lotus, whose pair of lotus hands is resplendent with a lotus each (and) whose excellent bath (is poured from) golden jars which are held by the trunks of two female elephants'.

पद्मा पद्मासीना पद्मोज्ज्वलपाणिपद्मयुगला वः।
प्रीत्या पश्यतु करिणीकरधृतकनकघटसुस्नाना।।

(Padmā Padāsīnā padmōjjvala – pāṇi – padma – yugalā vaḥ, prītyā paśyatu kariṇī - karadhṛita – kanaka – ghaṭa – susnānā)

Pārvatī

Similarly, only the Kaśākuḍi plates,[99] among all the Pallava epigraphs, has a verse invoking the grace of Pārvatī and runs as follows:

'May that blessed Āryā (Pārvatī), the sister of Vishṇu, instantly remove dire adversity, whom Cupid does not approach, out of fear, it seems because he has observed the (third) eye on (her) forehead (and therefore mistakes her) for Iśvara'.

दृष्ट्वा ललाटे नयनं भियेव कामो न यामीश्वर इत्युपास्ते।
विष्णोः स्वसा सा भगवत्यलक्ष्मीमार्या कदार्या क्षिणुतात् क्षणेन।।

(dṛishtva lalāṭē nayanam bhiyēva kāmō nayāmīśvara ityupāstē Vishnōḥ, svasā sā Bhagavatī alakshmīm aryā kadāryā kshinutāt kshaṇēna).

Echoes from Sanskrit Literature

The poets of the Sanskrit inscriptions of Tamil Nadu were gifted with extraordinary imagination and versatility. They were great scholars in Sanskrit and in the ancient texts and their works of prose and poetry are among the best in the Sanskrit literature of Tamil Nadu.

An indepth study of their works reveals that these poets were greatly influenced by the Sanskrit works such as the *Rāmāyaṇa* of Vālmiki, the works of Kālidāsa, especially the *Raghuvaṁśa* and other texts. Ravikīrti, the author of the famous Aihoḷe inscription of Chālukya Pulakēsin II (c. 634 A.D.) openly states at the end of this record that by his poetic skill he had attained to the fame of Kālidāsa and Bhāravi.

स विजयतां रविकीर्तिः कविताश्रित कालिदासभारविकीर्त्तिः
(sa vijayatām Ravikīrttiḥ kavitāsrita KālidāsaBhāravi kīrtiḥ).[100]

This poet who proclaims outright his admiration for Kalidāsa and Bhāravi was greatly influenced by the former's style, and there are many lines in the Aihoḷe inscription, which run parallel to Kālidāsa's *Raghuvaṁśa.*

Many of the poets who composed the inscriptions of the Pallava kings, must have been contemporaries of Ravikīrti, but unlike this poet they have not openly expressed their administration for these eminent Sanskrit composers of the past. However, there is unmistakable proof of the influence of these poets on those who composed the Pallava epigraphs and many verses and lines in the inscriptions run parallel, if not identical to the *Rāmāyaṇa* and the *Raghuvaṁśa.*

Even in some of the very early copper-plate grants of the Pallava kings, traces of this influence can be seen. In the Pikira plates of Siṁhavarman[101] (c. 5th century A.D., Guntur district, Andhra Pradesh), the line:

देवद्विज गुरु वृद्धोपचायिनः

(dēva dvija guru vṛiddhōpachāyinaḥ)

is clearly borrowed from the *Rāmāyaṇa* of Vālmiki:

बहुश्रुतानां वृद्धानां ब्राह्मणानां उपासितः

(bahuśrutānām vṛiddhānām brāhmaṇānām upāsitaḥ)[102]

A line in the *Raghuvaṁśa,* mentions that the Gods (dēvas) went to Lord Vishṇu just as travellers afflicted by heat seek a tree affording shade.

अभिजग्मुः निधागार्थ छायावृक्षमिवाध्वगाः।

(abhijagmuḥ nidhāgārtha chhāya vṛiksham iva adhvaghāḥ)[103]

And, this is compressed in one of the short titles (*birudas*) of king Rājasiṁha found in the Kailāsanātha temple in Kañchīpuram:

छाया वृक्षः

chhāyā vṛikshaḥ (the shading tree)[104]

Again, one of the 7th century epigraphs of

Narasiṁhavarman I at Māmallapuram lists one of his birudas 'Satyaparākramaḥ'[105] (one who is truly valorous) and this is one of the epithets frequently used by Vālmikī to describe Rāma

दिव्यैर्गुणैः शक्रसमो रामः सत्यपराक्रमः।
तमेवं गुणसंपन्नं रामं सत्यपराक्रम्।

'divyaiḥ guṇaiḥ Śakrasamō Rāmaḥ satyaparākramaḥ'[106] and *'tamēvam guṇasampannam Rāmam satyaprākramam'*[107]

In the Kuram plates of Paramēśvaravarman, the Goddess of victory is described as seated on the swing of doubt about mutual victory or defeat.

अन्योन्य जय पराजय सन्देह प्रेंखलग्न लक्ष्मी विहिते।

(anyōnya jaya parājaya sandēha prēṅkha-lagna Lakshmī vihitē)[108]

and this is reminiscent of the line in the *Raghuvaṁśa:*

'Since each side was victorious from time to time, the Goddess of victory indecisively stood between them'.

जयश्रींरन्तरा वेदि मत्तबारणयोरिव
विक्रम व्यतिहारेण सामान्योभूत् द्वयोरपि

(jayaśrīrantarā vēdi mattha vāraṇayoriva,
vikrama vyatihārēṇa sāmānyōbhūt dvayōrapi).[109]

Again, this poet of the Kūram charter mentions that 'the disc of the sun was caused to assume the likeness of the moon through the mist of dust that was produced by the marching of his (Paramēśvaravarman's) army:

रेणु तुहिनेव आरोपित शशिमण्डल सादृश्य सहस्रकर विंबे।

(rēṇu-tuhinēna ārōpita śaśi-maṇḍala
sādriśya sahasra-karabimbē)[110]

and this appears to have been certainly drawn again from the *Raghuvaṁśa*, where Kālidāsa, describes an expedition of king Aja thus:

'the dust that is raised by the horses obscures the flashing lusture of the crest gems of other princes.'

कुर्वन्ति सामन्त शिखामणीनां प्रभाप्ररोहास्तमयं रजांसि।
(*kurvanti sāmanta śikhāmaṇīnām prabhā prarōha astamayam rajāmsi*).[111]

or even more likely, from another place in the *Raghuvaṁśa* where Rāma is described as going on an expedition and 'eclipsing the Sun's rays with his army's dust'

सैन्य रेणु मुषितार्कदीधितिः
(*sainya-rēṇu mushitārka dīdhitiḥ*)[112]

In yet another place in the Kūram inscription, this composer, who was obviously very fascinated by the *Raghuvaṁśa*, describes Narasimhavarman I as one, who like a thousand-armed Kārtavīrya had, as it were, a thousand arms, experiencing fight in hundreds of battles.

सहस्रबाहु इव समरशत निर्विष्ट सहस्रवाहु कर्मणः
(*sahasra bāhu iva samara śata nirvishṭa sahasra bāhu karmaṇaḥ*)[113]

and this has been bodily incorporated into this inscription from the *Raghuvaṁśa* which describes Kārtavīrya as one 'who had a thousand arms experiencing fight in battle, and who had fixed sacrificial posts in the eighteen continents.

संग्राम निर्विष्ट सहस्रबाहु रष्टादशद्वीप निखात यूपः
(*sangrāma nirvishṭa sahasra bāhu rashtādaśa dvīpa nikhāta yūpaḥ*).[114]

In the Kaśākuḍi plates of Nandivarman II Pallavamalla, the poet composer Trivikrama starts this record with the benediction:

'victorious is the supreme Brahman, which is the cause of the production, stability and destruction of the whole world'.

जगत्त्रयजन्मस्थिति संहृति कारणं परब्रह्म
(*jagat traya janma sthiti samhṛiti kāraṇam para brahma*)[115]

and this is very similar to the wordings of the *Taittirīya*

Upanishad, 'the Brahman is that from which the world is produced, sustained and absorbed again'

यतो वा इमानि भूतानि जायन्ते, येन जातानि जीवन्ति
यत्प्रयन्त्यभिसंविशन्ति, तत् ब्रह्म।

(yatō vā imāni bhūtāni jāyantē yēna jātāni jīvanti
yat prayantyabhi samviśanti tad Brahma).[116]

In one of the other invocatory verses in the Kaśākuḍi plates in praise of Lord Gaṇēśa, the poet describes this deity as one who is 'as white as the Kailāsa (mountain) and has a huge serpent as a girdle'.

कैलासगौरः पृथुनाग कक्ष्यः

(Kailāsagauraḥ pṛithunāgakakshyaḥ)[117]

and this too, is very similar to the line in the *Raghuvaṁśa:*

'of Śiva desirous of mounting his bull, white as the mountain Kailāsa'

कैलास गौरं वृषभारुरोहो

(Kailāsagauram vṛishabhāruruhō)[118]

Again in the Kaśākuḍi plates, the lines in which the Pallava kings are described using the technical points of grammar (as mentioned earlier in this chapter), such as *prakṛiti* and *pratyaya*[119] seems to be an echo of a verse in the *Raghuvaṁśa* which describes the wedding of Daśaratha's sons with Janaka's daughters 'as the union of the base *(prakṛiti)* with affix *(pratyaya).*

प्रत्ययप्रकृतियोगसन्निभः

(pratyaya-prakṛiti-yōga-sannibhaḥ)[120]

The Taṇḍantōṭṭam copper-plate grant again belonging to the period of Nandivarman II Pallavamalla, composed by a poet named Paramēśvara, surnamed Uttarakāraṇika, contains a verse resembling the *'Raghuvaṁśa.* At the beginning of this record, this composer describes

Nandivarman II as one in whom Lakshmī dwells permanently, abandoning her vice of fickleness.

श्रीश्च यस्मिन्निवसति सुचिरन् त्यक्त चापल्य दोषा

(śrīscha yasmin nivasati suchiran tyakta chāpalya dōshā)[121]

and this is very much like a verse in *Raghuvaṁśa* 'although fickle by nature, the Goddess of Prosperity dwelt with him firmly',

प्रसादाभि मुखे तस्मिंश्चपलापिस्वभावतः।
निकषे हेमरेखेव श्रीरासीत् अनपायिनी।।

(prasādāpbhi mukhē tasminśchapalāpi svabhāvataḥ,
nikashē hēmarēkhēva Śrīrāsīt anapayinī)[122]

Another verse in the *Raghuvaṁśa* in which king Dilīpa is described as one who 'combined knowledge with restraint of speech, might with forgiveness, generosity with absence of gloriousness; his virtues, thus being associated with other virtues seemed to be twin born'.

ज्ञाने मौनं क्षमा शक्तौ त्यागे श्लाघाविपर्ययः
गुणा गुणानुवन्धित्वात्तस्य सप्रसवा इव

jñānē mounam kshamā śaktau tyāgē ślāgā viparyayaḥ,
guṇā guṇānubandhitvāt tasya sa prasavā iva)[123]

seems to have caught the fancy of the poet named Mahēśvara Manōdhīra, composer of the Vēlūrpāḷayam copper-plate grant of Nandivarman III who praises the king's subjects in a similar manner as Kāḷidāsa thus:

'men of high birth with qualities, women with morality, millionaires with charity, humility with knowledge'.

गुणैः कुलभुवः शीलेन वामेक्षणा, त्यागेनार्थपतिः श्रुतेन विनयः

(guṇaiḥ kula-bhuvaḥ śīlēna vāmēkshaṇā tyāgēna arthapatiḥ śrutēna vinayaḥ)[124]

The poet Nāgaya, the composer of the *praśasti* of the Bāhūr inscription of Nṛipatuṅga, praises a chieftain named Mārtāṇḍa in a very poetic manner as being 'an ornament to the world like the moon and resembling the ocean in profundity'

शशिवत्तिलको लोके गाम्भीर्यादेस्समुद्रवत्

(śaśivat tilakō lōkē gambhīryādēssmudravat)[125]

And this seems to be an echo from the Vālmīki Rāmāyaṇa where Lord Rāma is described as 'being majestic like the ocean' (*samudra iva gāmbīryē*) and 'very pleasing like the moon' (*sōmavat priyadarshanaḥ*)[126].

समुद्र इव गाम्भीर्ये, सोमवत् प्रियदर्शनः

Meters used in the Pallava Inscriptions

1. *Paḷḷankōvil plates of Simhavarman* (c. 550 A.D.) v.1-Upajāti; v.2 Śārdūlavikriḍitā; v.3-Pṛithvī; v.4-Indravajrā; v.5-Śārdūlavikrīḍitā; v.6-Indravajrā; vv.7, 8 and 9 – Anushṭubh
2. *Kūram plates of Paramēśvaravarman I* v.1-Śragdharā; vv.2 and 3 - Śārdūlavikrīḍitā; v.4-Anushṭubh; vv.5-9 & 21-Āryā; v.10 Sugitī; vv.11, 16 19-Āryagīti; vv.13, 20, 24 – Gitī; v.-15-Lalitā; v.22 – Vasantatilakā; vv.23 & 38 – Mālinī.
3. *Inscription of Paramēśvara I in Gaṇēsha* rock-cut temple and Dhar-marāja maṇḍapa, Māmallampuram vv.1-10 – Anushṭubh : v.11 - Āryā
4. *Kailāsanātha temple inscription of Rājasimha* vv.1-5 - Śragdharā; v.6 Pṛithvī; vv.7-8 - Śārdūlavikrīḍitā; v.9 – Pṛithvī
5. *Kailāsanātha temple inscription of Raṅgapatākā* vv.1-2 – Vasantatilakā; v.3 – Anushṭubh
6. *Śāluvankuppam inscription of Rājasimha* vv.1-4 Anushṭubh; v. 6 - Śragdharā; v.7 - Āryā.
7. *Udayēndiram plates of Nandivarman II Pallavamalla* (c. 752 A.D.)
   v.1 – not clear; vv.2, 3 & 6 – Vasantatilakā; v.4 – Jagati – Indravaṁśā; v.5 –Bṛihati; v.7 – Anushṭubh;

8 *Kaśākuḍi plates of Nandivarman II Pallavamalla* (c. 753-54 A.D.) vv.1, 5, & 16 –; v.2 Indravamśa; vv.3, 4, 8, 11, 12, 25, 29 - Śārdūlavikriḍitā; vv.6, 7, 14, 18 & 19 – Indravajra; v.10 – Mālinī; vv.13, 15, 17, 22, 23, 24, 26 & 27 - Vasantatīlakā; vv.20, 31-34 – Anushṭubh; v.21 Upēndravajra; vv.28 & 30 - Śragdharā.

9 *Pullūr plates of Nandivarman II Pallavamalla* (c. 764-65 A.D.) vv.1, 3 & 4 – Anushṭubh; v.2 - Śragdharā; vv. 5 & 6 - Śārdūlavikrīḍitā

10 *Taṇḍantōṭṭam plates of Nandivarman II Pallavamalla* (c. 789 A.D.)
v.1 – Upajāti; v.2 Mandākrāntā; vv. 3, 9 & 11 – Vasantatilakā; v.4 - Śragdharā; vv.5, 10, 12, & 13 - Śārdūlavikrīḍitā; vv.6, 8, & 14 - Āryā; v.7 – Prithvī

11 *Paṭṭaṭāḷmaṅgalam plates of Nandivarman II Pallavamalla* (c. 792 A.D.)
v.1 Śikhariṇī; vv.2, 3, 6 & 10 - Śārdūlavikrīḍitā; vv.4 & 5 – Indravajra; v.7 – Praharshiṇī; v.8. – Pushpitāgrā; v.9 – Rathōddhatā and v.11 - Āryā

12 *Vēlūrpāḷayam plates of Nandivarman III* (c. 852 A.D.)
vv.1, 2, 3, 17, 18 & 21 Śārdūlavikrīḍitā; vv.4, 5, 6, 9, 11, 13, 16, 23, 24 & 26 – Upajāti; vv.7, 12, 14, 25, 27 & 28 – Anushṭubh; v.8 Upēndravajra; v.10 – Pṛithvī; v.15 – Viyōginī; v.19 – Indravajra; v.20 Vasantatilakā; v.22 - Śragdharā

13 *Kumaraḍimaṅgalam plates of Nandivarman III*
vv.1 & 6 Mandākrāntā; vv.2 & 4 Śārdūlavikrīḍitā; vv. 3 & 7 – Mālinī; v.5 - Āryā.

14 *Chiṟṟūr plates of Nṛipatuṅgavarman* (c. 875 A.D.)
vv. 1, 7, 8 & 13 Śārdūlavikrīḍitā; vv. 2 & 7 - Śragdharā; v.4 – Indravajrā; vv.3 & 5 Rathōddhata; vv. 6, 9, 10, 16- Vamśasta; vv .11 & 12 – Vasantatilakā; v.14 – Upēndravajrā; vv.15, 18 - Āryā; v.19 Anushṭubh

15 *Bāhūr plates of Nṛipatuṅgavarman (c. 877 A.D.)*
vv. 1 & 7 Drutavilambitā; vv.15 & 31 – Vasantatilakā; v.32 - Āryā; vv.3-6, 8-14 & 16-30 – Anushṭubh

16 *Vēḷāñjēri plates of Aparājita* (c. 878 A.D.)
vv. 1, 5, 12, 13 – Vasantatilakā; v.2 – Praharśiṇī; vv. 3 & 10 Śārdūlavikrīḍitā; vv. 4 & 7 – Rathōddhata; vv.6, 8, 11, 14, & 15 – Upēndravajrā; v.9 – Kāmamatta.

REFERENCES

1. *Mattavilāsaprahasana,* Edited by N.P. Unni, Trivandrum, 1974.
2. Michael Lockwood and Vishnu Bhatt (Ed. and Tr.), *King Mahēndravarman's Plays,* Madras, 1991.
3. *S.I.I.,* Vol. I, No.25, pp. 17-18.
4. T.V. Mahalingam, *Inscriptions of the Pallavas,* New Delhi, 1988, p. 209.
5. *S.I.I.,* Vol. II, No. 73, v. 29, p. 350 (Kaśākuḍi plates)
6. *S.I.I.,* Vol. II, No. 74, *l.*27, p. 365 (Udayēndiram plates)
7. *Ibid.*
8. *E.I.,* Vol. XXXII, No. 2, pp. 89-90 (Mañchikallu inscription)
9. *E.I.,* Vol. I, No.1, pp. 5-6 (Hīrahadagalli inscription)
10. *E.I.,* Vol. VI, No. 8, pp. 86-88 (Maidavōlu inscription)
11. *E.I.,* Vol. VIII, No.12, pp.145-146 (British Museum plates of Chārūdēvī)
12. *E.I.,* Vol. XV, No.11-A, pp. 251-52 (Oṁgōḍu I plates)
13. *I.A.,* (Feb.,1876), No. XII, pp. 51-52 (Uruvapaḷḷi plates)
14. T.V. Mahalingam, *op.cit.,* pp. 49-51 (Neḍungarāya plates)
15. N. Ramesan, Vēsanta Grant of Pallava Siṁhavarman, *TASSI,* 1962, pp.95-96.
16. *E.I.,* Vol. XXXVIII, No.18, pp.104-105 (Sakrēpaṭna plates)
17. *E.I.,* Vol. VIII, No. 23, pp. 234-235.
18. *E.I.,* Vol. XV, No.11-B, pp. 254-255 (Oṁgōḍu II plates)
19. *E.I.,* Vol. VIII, No.15, pp. 161-162 (Pikira plates)
20. *E.I.,* Vol. XXIV, No.43, pp. 301-303 (Viḷāvaṭṭi plates)
21. *E.I.,* Vol. XXIV, No.18, pp. 141-142 (Chura plates)
22. *E.I.,* Vol. III, No. 23, pp. 145-147 (Udayēndiram plates of Nandivarman I)

23. T.N. Subramaniam, *The Paḷḷankōvil Jaina copper-plate Grant of Early Pallava Period, TASSI*, Vol. IV, pp.75-80.
24. *E.I.*, Vol. XII, No. 27, p. 225 (Daḷavanūr inscription)
25. *E.I.*, Vol. IV, No. 19, p.153 (Mahēndravāḍi inscription)
26. *S.I.I.*, Vol. IV, No. 136, p.12 (Māmaṇḍūr inscription)
27. *E.I.*, Vol. XVII, No. 5, p.17 (Maṇḍagapaṭṭu inscription)
28. *E.I.*, Vol. XII, No. 13, pp.7-8 (Pallāvaram inscription)
29. *S.I.I.*, Vol. I, Nos. 33 and 34, pp.29-30 (Tiruchirāpaḷḷi inscriptions)
30. *E.I.*, Vol. XII, No. 28, pp. 231-236 (Kuḍimiyāmalai inscription)
31. *S.I.I.*, Vol. XII, No.7-A, p. 3.
32. *S.I.I.*, Vol. I, No.1, pp. 148-152 (Kūram copper-plates of Paramēśvaravarman I).
33. *S.I.I.*, Vol. I, No.18, p. 4.
34. *S.I.I.*, Vol. I, No.19, p. 6.
35. *S.I.I.*, Vol. I, No. 24, pp. 12-13.
36. *S.I.I.*, Vol. I, No. 21, pp. 6-7.
37. *S.I.I.*, Vol. II, No. 74, pp. 365-370 (Udayēndiram plates).
38. *S.I.I.*, Vol. II, No. 73, pp. 346-353 (Kaśākuḍi plates).
39. *E.I*, Vol. XXXVI, No. 20, pp. 152-158 (Pullūr plates).
40. *S.I.I.*, Vol. II, No. 99, pp. 520-528 (Taṇḍantōṭṭam plates).
41. *E.I.*, Vol. XVIII , No.14, pp. 120-122 (Paṭṭaṭāḷmaṅgalam plates).
42. N. Ramesan, *The Kumāraḍimaṅgalam plates of the Pallava King Nandivarma III* from *Sri Mallampalli Somasekhara Sarma Commemoration Volume*, Hyderabad, 1976, pp.200-205.
43. *S.I.I.*, Vol. II, No. 98, pp. 507-510 (Vēlūrpāḷayam plates).
44. T.V. Mahalingam, *op.cit.*, pp. 439-450 (Chiṟṟūr plates of Nṛipatuṅgavarman).
45. *E.I.*, Vol. XVIII, No.2, pp. 9-12 (Bāhūr plates of Nṛipatuṅgavarman).
46. R. Nagaswamy, *TVCP*, Madras, 1978.
47. C. Minakshi, *Administration and Social Life under the Pallavas*, Madras, 1977, pp. 14-15.
48. R. Narasimhachar, Bāmaha and Daṇḍi, *I.A.* (1912) p. 92.
49. R. Gopalan, *History of the Pallavas of Kanchi*, Madras, 1928, pp. 110-111
50. T.N. Subramaniam, *op.cit.* v. 9, p. 76

51. Kaśākuḍi plates, *op.cit.*, v. 31, p. 351.
52. Udayēndiram plates, *op.cit.*, v. 8, p. 370.
53. Taṇḍantōṭṭam plates, *op.cit.*, v.14, p. 521
54. C. Minakshi, *op.cit.*, p. 78
55. T.N. Subramaniam, *op.cit.*, p. 74
56. Vēlūrpāḷayam plates, *op.cit.*, v.28, p. 509.
57. Bāhūr plates, *op.cit.*, v. 30, p. 11
58. T.V. Mahalingam, *op.cit.*, p. 442
59. R. Nagaswamy: *TVCP*, v.19, Plate V, p.1
60. R. Nagaswamy, *The Chiṟṟūr Copper-Plates of Nṛipatuṅga* from *'Studies in Ancient Tamil Law and Society'* by R. Nagaswamy, Madras, 1978, p. 37
61. T.N. Subramaniam, *op.cit.*, v. 5, p. 76
62. *S.I.I.*, Vol. I, Nos. 33 and 34, pp. 29-30
63. P.R. Srinivasan, *Gangādharāshṭakam in Pallava Inscription from Tiruchirāpaḷḷi* from *Śrīnidhiḥ* (Shri K.R. Srinivasan Festschrift), Madras, 1983, p. 434
64. Kūram plates, *op.cit.*
65. *S.I.I.*, Vol. I, No.18, pp. 4-5
66. *Ibid.*, No.19, p. 6
67. *S.I.I.*, Vol. XII, No. 28.
68. *S.I.I.*, Vol. I, No. 24, pp.12-13.
69. *E.I.*, Vol. XIX, No. 18-B, pp.109-15.
70. S. Sankaranarayanan, A Pallava Inscriptional Poem in Sanskrit, *ALB*, Vol. 55, 1991, pp. 72-73
71. *Ibid.*
72. *Ibid.*, pp. 77-78
73. Udayēndiram plates, *op. cit.*, p. 366
74. *Ibid.*, v. 4, p. 367
75. Kaśākuḍi plates, *op. cit.*, v. 9, pp. 346-47
76. *Ibid.*, v. 24, p. 349
77. *Ibid.*, pp. 348
78. *Ibid.*, v. 20, p. 347-348
79. *Ibid.*, line 96, p. 351.
80. Taṇḍantōṭṭam plates, *op.cit.*, v. 4
81. *Ibid.*, v. 12, p. 520

82. Kaśākuḍi plates, *op.cit.*, v. 2, p. 346
83. Paṭṭaṭāḷmaṅgalam plates, *op.cit.*, v. 1, p. 120
84. Bāhūr plates, *op.cit.*, v. 1, p. 9
85. R. Nagaswamy, TCVP (Vēḷāñjēri plates of Aparājita), v.1, plate I, p.2
86. *S.I.I.*, Vol. I, No. 18, v. 1, p. 4
87. *Ibid.*, No.19, p.6.
88. Kūram plates, *op. cit.*, v. 1, p. 148
89. Udayēndiram plates, *op. cit.*, v. 1, pp. 365-66
90. Kaśākuḍi plates, *op.cit.*, v. 3, p. 346
91. Vēlūrpāḷayam plates, *op.cit.*, v. 2, p. 507
92. R. Nagaswamy, *TVCP* (Vēḷāñjēri plates of Aparājita), V.2.
93. Kaśākuḍi plates, *op. cit.*, v. 7, p. 346
94. K.K. Pillay, *A Social History of the Tamils*, Madras, 1969, p. 158
95. Kaśākuḍi plates, *op.cit.*, v. 1, p. 346
96. Vēlūrpāḷayam plates, *op.cit.*, v. 1, p. 507
97. Paṭṭaṭāḷmaṅgalam plates, *op.cit.*, v. 2, p. 120
98. Kaśākuḍi plates, *op.cit.*, v. 5, p. 346
99. *Ibid.*, v. 6
100. *E.I.*, Vol. VI, No. 1, p. 7
101. *E.I.*, Vol. VIII, No. 15, p. 161
102. *Śrīmad Vālmīki Rāmāyaṇam*, II.2.33; C. Sivaramamurti, *Epigraphical Echos of Kālidāsa*, Madras, 1944, p. 6
103. V. Venkataraghavachariar (Ed.) *Raghuvaṁśa Mahākāvya*, Madras, 1991, X. 5
104. *S.I.I.*, Vol. I, No.25, p. 18; C. Sivaramamurti, *op.cit.*, p. 7
105. *S.I.I.*, Vol. I, No.1, p. 4
106. *Śrīmad Vālmīki Rāmāyaṇam*, II.2.28
107. *Ibid.*, I. 1.19; see also C. Sivaramamurti, *op.cit.*, p. 9
108. Kūram plates, *op.cit.*, lines 33-34
109. *Raghuvaṁśa, op.cit.*, VI. 33
110. Kūram plates, *op.cit*, line 23, p.148
111. *Raghuvaṁśa*, VI.33
112. *Ibid.*, XI.51
113. Kūram plates, *op.cit.*, p. 148
114. *Raghuvaṁśa*, VI.38; C. Sivaramamurti, *op.cit.*, p. 29

115. Kaśākuḍi plates, *op.cit.*, v. 1, p. 346
116. *Upanishadsaṁgrahaḥ* (Ed) by J.L. Shastri, Delhi, 1984, III.1.1.
117. Kaśākuḍi plates, *op.cit.*, v. 7, p. 346
118. *Raghuvaṁśa*, II.35; see also C. Sivaramamurti, *op.cit.*, p. 89
119. Kaśākuḍi plates, *op.cit.*, p. 348.
120. *Raghuvaṁśa*, XI.56
121. Taṇḍantōṭṭam plates, *op.cit.*, v. 4, p. 520
122. *Raghuvaṁśa*, *op.cit.*, XVII.46
123. *Ibid.*, I.22
124. Vēlūrpāḷayam plates, *op.cit.*, v. 21, p. 508
125. Bāhūr plates, *op.cit.*, v.19, p.515
126. *Śrīmad Vālmīki Rāmāyaṇam*, Sarga I, 17 & 18

2

Pāṇḍya Period

The Pāṇḍyan rulers, like the Pallava kings, were themselves highly literate and patronized poets and other learned men of their land. Māravarman Rājasimha I is described as 'an ornament of learning' (*vidyāchāra vibhushaṇah*), and also as a 'depository of sacred knowledge' (*śrutadhārah*) in the Sanskrit portion of the Veḷvikuḍi charter.[1] A certain Sundara Pāṇḍya is called very poetically as' a helmsman in the ocean of all *śāstras*' (*samasta-śāstrārṇava karṇadhārō yadudbhavaḥ Sundara Pāṇḍya-nāmaḥ*) in the Larger Siṇṇamaṇūr copper-plates.[2] It is thus not surprising that these scholar-kings encouraged many poets and commissioned them to compose their royal charters.

The earliest Pāṇḍyan epigraph written in Sanskrit is the one found at Āṇaimalai (near Madurai), dated 770 A.D. of the period of Jaṭila Parāntaka Neḍuñjaḍaiyaṇ alias Varaguṇa I.[3] This inscription consists of only three verses composed in the Āryā and Vaṁśastha metres.

The next known Sanskrit inscription of the Pāṇḍyan period is found at Tirupparaṅkuṇṛam (near Madurai) and also belongs to the reign of Varaguṇa I.[4] This epigraph, which consists of only one verse, is written in *śragdhara* metre.

Although these two records are very important from the view-point of history, yet they do not contain much by way of literary merit. It is only the copper-plate inscriptions of the Pāṇḍyas which truly reflect the talent and scholarship of the poets who composed them. These copper-plate records, like those of the Pallava period are bi-lingual and the focus of this chapter will be on the Sanskrit *praśasti* sections of these inscriptions.

The copper-plate epigraphs which have been analyzed in this chapter are the Vēḷvikuḍi plates of Pāṇḍyan Neḍuṇjaḍaiyaṉ (c. 770 A.D.),[5] the Śrīvarmaṅgalam plates also of Neḍuṇjaḍaiyaṉ (c. 785 A.D.), [6] Daḷavāypuram plates of Parāntaka Vīra-Nārāyaṇa (c. 910 A.D.),[7] Larger Siṉṉamaṉūr plates of Rājasiṁha II (c. 926-927 A.D.)[8] and the Śivakāśi plates of Vīra-Pāṇḍya (c. 940-41 A.D.).[9]

In addition to this, a long and beautiful inscription of the reign of Jaṭāvarman Sundara-Pāṇḍya I of the 13th century A.D. inscribed on a wall of the Raṅganāthasvāmi temple at Śrīraṅgam (Tiruchirāpaḷḷi district)[10] consisting of thirty verses in very chaste language has also been taken up for study in this chapter.

Poets of the Pāṇḍyan Inscriptions

Many of the copper-plate epigraphs of the kings of the Pāṇḍya dynasty, like those of the Pallava kings provide the names of the poets who composed these royal documents. From a study of these inscriptions, as well as from the details which they give about themselves, it is clear that these poets were great scholars in Sanskrit and well-read in Vedic and Puranic lore.

The earliest copper-plate grant which mentions the name of the poet-composer is the Vēḷvikkuḍi epigraph of Pāṇḍyan Neḍuṇjaḍaiyaṉ. A line in Tamil at the conclusion of the Sanskrit section of this charter gives his name as

Vārōdayabhaṭṭa and describes him as 'a performer of all sacrifices'.[11]

The Daḷavāypuram plates mention that the *praśasti* of this inscription was written by Mādhavakavi, who is described as 'being of good speech, living at Śrīvallabhamaṅgalam, an adept in the scriptures' and other details about his family.

यं योगेश्वर भट्टं अष्टधरणीदेवेश्वरभ्रातरं
विद्यावृत्तनिधिं विदुर्गुणनिधेः पुत्रं गणस्वामिनः।
तत्पुत्रस्य मुखात्प्रशस्तिरुदिता तीर्थस्य शास्त्रेष्वियं
यश्श्रीवल्लभमङ्गले वसतिमान् वाग्मी कविर्माधवः।।

(*yam yogēśvara-bhaṭṭam ashṭadharaṇī-dēvēśvara-bhrātaram*
vidya-vṛitta-nidhim vidhurguṇa nidēḥ putram Gaṇasvāminaḥ,
tatputrasya mukhāt prasastir uditā tīrtthasya śastreshviyam
yaḥ Śrīvallabhamaṅgaḷē vasatimān vāgmī kavir Mādhavaḥ[12])

The Larger Sinnamaṉūr copper-plate charter, in the very last verse of the Sanskrit section, states that 'Vāsudēva, a friend of a person named Maḍhuraguṇa, and the elder brother of Vishṇu, who had studied the whole (science of) literature and was the birth-place of modesty and intelligence, composed this matchless *praśasti*'

विदित सकल वाङ्मयस्य विष्णोर्विनयनयप्रभवस्य पूर्वजो यः
अरचयदतुलामिमां प्रशस्तिं मधुरगुणस्य सखा स वासुदेवः

(*vidita sakalavañmayasya Vishnōr-vinayanaya-prabhavasya pūrvajō yaḥ,*
arachayadatulāmimām praśastim Madhuraguṇasya sakhā sa Vāsudēvaḥ).[13]

According to the Śivakāśi inscription of Vīra-Pāṇḍya, a poet named Pārthivakēsari from a village named Antagrāma, who was the adviser to the king on *dharma*, son of the famous Vishṇutrāta, a treasure-house of learning, grandson of Ravi, a repository of good poetry and an equal to Bṛihaspati' was the author of the Sanskrit *praśasti* of this charter.

पौत्रस्सत्कवितास्पदस्य धिषणप्रख्यस्य योयं रवेः
विष्णुत्रातसमाह्वयः श्रुतनिधिर्यस्योरुकीर्तिः पिता।
अन्तर्ग्रामसमुद्भवस्य नृपतेर्द्धर्मोपदेष्टा गुरुः
श्रव्यां पार्थिव केसरी स कृतवान् एतां पशस्तिं कवेः।।

(pautrassatkavitāspadsya dhishaṇa-prakhyasya yōyam Ravēḥ,
Vishṇutrātasamāhvayaḥ sruta-nidhiryasyorukīrtiḥ pita,
Antargrāmā-samudbhavasya nṛipatērdharmōpadeshṭhā guruḥ,
śravyām Pārtthivakēsari sa kṛitavān ētām praśastim kavēh)[14]

It is a pity that the poets of the Sanskrit verses of the Śrīvaramaṅgalam and the Smaller Siṉṉamaṉūr copper-plate grants as well as the composer of the long lithic epigraph of Jaṭāvarman Sundara Pāṇḍya found in the Ranganāthasvāmi temple, Śrīraṅgam have not been mentioned in these records.

Literary Beauty found in the Pāṇḍyan Inscriptions

• In the Vēḷvikkuḍi copper-plate charter of Pāṇḍyan Neḍuñjaḍaiyaṉ, there is a fine example of *vṛityanuprāsa alaṅkāra* in verse twelve,

'Is he Nara, i.e. Arjuna, or a demon, is he Śiva or Vishṇu, or is he Indra, come with anger; thus thinking of him in the battlefield, the frightened king Pallavamalla runs away from him'

नरो नु रक्षो नु हरो नु पूरुषः परो नु शक्रोनु सरोषमागतः
इतिस्म मत्वा युधि यम्भयार्द्दितः पलायते पल्लवमल्ल भूपतिः।

(*Narōnu rakshōnu Harōnu pūrushaḥ, parōnu śakrōnu sarōsham āgataḥ*

iti sma matva yudhi yaṁ bhayārdditaḥ palāyatē Pallavamallą bhūpatiḥ).[15]

A few verses later, this poet gives a very beautiful poetic description of his king Neḍuñjaḍaiyaṉ in *mālabhāriṇī* metre, thus:

'I imagine he lent his virtues to the Kṛita Age, he lent to

the celestial tree, its nature from his hands; he lent protection to his subjects who sought refuge in him; and to his enemies, he gave heaven on the battlefield itself'.

कलये स गुणान् अदात्कृतस्य स्वभुजाभ्यां सुरपादपस्वभावं।
अभयं शरणागतप्रजाभ्यस्सदिवं संयति शत्रुपार्थिवेभ्यः।।

(kalayē sa guṇān adāt kṛitasya; sva-bhujābhyām sura-pādapa-svabhāvam,
abhayam śaraṇāgata-prajābhyas saḥ divam samyati śatru pārtivēbhyaḥ)[16]

In the Daḷavāypuram plates of Parāntaka Vīra-Nārāyaṇa Pāṇḍya, the poet of this charter, named Vāsudēva, praises this king, his patron in a very simple but beautiful manner thus:

'He, the younger brother of Varaguṇa was a fire to the wood-like enemies and moon to the lily-like friends and became the lord of the earth surrounded by the ocean'.

तस्यानुजो वह्निररिन्धनानां
श्रीवीरनारायण नामधेयः।
सोमोपमो मित्र कुमुद्वतीनां
नाथोऽभवद्वारिधि मेखलायाः।।

(tasyānujō vahnir arindhanānām
Śrī Vīranārāyaṇa nāmadhēyaḥ,
sōmōpamō mitra kumudvatīnām
nāthōbhavat vāridhi mēkhalāyāḥ)[17]

This above-mentioned verse in *Indravajra* metre, contains two *alaṅkāras*, namely *rūpaka* in *arindhanānām* and *upama* in *sōmōpamō*.

In the Larger Siṉṉamaṉūr copper-plate grant, there is a beautiful depiction of *vīra-rasa* in verse thirteen, wherein king Parāntaka Pāṇḍya is described as;

'Having captured in a battle near Kharagiri, the powerful (king) Ugra, who possessed a herd of strong elephants, whose tusks were red with the blood of enemy kings with an army (which was) the sword (held) in hand'.

खरगिरिमभितः करन्द्रियूथं
रिपुनृप शोणित शोणिदन्तमाजौ।
करकलित कृपाण मात्र सैन्यस्सरभस-
मुग्रमुदग्रमग्रहीत्यः।।

(*Kharagirimabhitaḥ karandriyūtham*
ripunṛipa śōṇitaśōṇidantam ājau,
kharakalitakṛipāṇamātra sainyassarabhasa-
mugramudagram-agrahītyaḥ).[18]

In the Larger Siṉṉamaṉūr copper-plate inscription, the poet Vāsudēva praises king Rājasiṁha Pāṇḍya and gives full vent to his powers of imagination in *vasantatilakā* metre and in *samuchchaya alaṅkāra* thus:

'The requests of all supplicants are not enough for (i.e. to satisfy) his liberality; nor his enemies for his prowess; nor all the worlds for (his) lustrous fame; nor (again) the words of the master of words (i.e. Bṛihaspati), for praising (his) virtues'.

नालं भवन्ति निखिलार्त्थि जनाभिलाषाः
त्यागस्य यस्य रिपवोपि पराक्रमस्य।
कीर्त्तेसमस्त भुवनानि समुल्लसन्त्या
वाचस्पतेरपि वचांसि गुणस्तुतीनाम्।।

(*nālam bhavanti nikhilārtthi janā-bhilāshāḥ*
tyāgasya yasya ripavaḥ api parākramasya
kīrtēḥ samasta bhuvanāni samullasantyā
Vāchaspatēr api vachāmsi guṇastutīnām)[19]

The Śivakāśi copper-plate charter of Vīra-Pāṇḍya also contains some stanzas of literary beauty, in one of which the composer describes Vīra-Pāṇḍya as follows:

'He with matchless excellence pleases the world with his qualities; his subjects with his pleasant deeds; *brāhmaṇas* with gifts; enemies with harm; relatives with pleasure and supplicants with their objects of desire'

विश्वं गुणोघैः जनताः प्रमोदैरर्थैर्द्विजेन्द्रान् अहितानन्नार्थैः।
वन्धून् सुखेराश्रयतोऽभिलाषै र्यः पूरयत्य प्रतिमप्रभावः।।

(viśvam guṇōgaiḥ janatāḥ pramōdair artthair dvijēndrānāhitān anārtthaiḥ,

bandhūn sukhairāśrayatōabhilāshair yaḥ pūrayati apratima prabhāvaḥ).[20]

An inscription of Jaṭāvarman Sundara-Pāṇḍya I engraved on the east wall of the second *prākāra* of the Raṅganāthasvāmi temple in Śrīraṅgam is a beautiful Sanskrit poem, in which the poet lists the various benefactions made by this king to this hoary temple-complex. Each verse, which mentions a gift, brims over with poetic imagination and is couched in excellent Sanskrit.

In one of the verses, this composer states, 'the king, who was the lord of the world, made at Śrīraṅga, a golden tower (*gōpuram*) which was the residence of Narasiṁha (and) which surpassed the splendour of the peaks of (the golden mountain) Sumēru. When at night, the full moon stood over this tower (*gōpuram*) which emitted a mass of bright light, it looked as though the moon had joined the sun'.

प्रत्यादिष्टसुमेरुशृङ्गविभवं विश्वोत्तरक्ष्मापतिः
श्रीरङ्गे नरसिंहधामविदधे कार्त्तस्वरं गोपुरं।
यस्मिन्नक्तमुदीर्णभासुरमहत्सोमे मुहूर्तं गतः
पर्याप्ता कृतिरेव भास्करमिव प्राप्तश्शशी दृश्यते।।

(pratyādishṭa sumēru-sṛingavibhavam viśvōttara kshmāpatiḥ Śrīraṅgē Narasiṁha-dhāma vidadhē kārttasvaram gōpuram,

yasmin nakta -mudīrṇa bhāsuramahassōmē muhūrtam gataḥ paryāptā kṛitirēva bhāskaramiva prāptas śaśī dṛiśyatē).[21]

Yet another verse of this inscription mentions:

'In the month of *Chaitra,* the sun among kings celebrated for Raṅgin, the procession-festival, which is praiseworthy on account of bright, wonderful and prosperous days. It is no wonder that those who possess intelligence, rejoice, when even the trees, which are devoid of intelligence, are in high glee (or in full bloom).

चैत्रेमासि चकार राजतपनो यात्रोत्सवं रङ्गिनः
श्लाघां कान्तिमयैः तथाद्भुतमयैस्सम्पन्मयै वासरैः।
नन्दन्त्येव हि तेन विस्मयपदं ये बिभ्रते चेतनां
अचैतन्यमृतोपि यत्र दधते वृक्षा विकासम्परम्।।

(Chaitrē māsi chakāra rājatapanō yātrōtsavam Raṅginaḥ
ślagham kāntimayais tathā adbhutamayais
sampan-mayair vāsaraiḥ,
nandantyēva hi tena vismayapadam yē bibhratē chētanām
achaitanyabhṛitōpi yatra dadhatē vṛikshā vikāsam param).[22]

In another verse in this inscription, the composer refers to the *viśvarūpa* aspect of Lord Vishṇu when he mentions that Sundara Pāṇḍya offered food to Lord Raṅganātha 'which even the fourteen worlds had been unable to fill'

संपूर्णं विदधे गभीरमुदरंरंगेशितुशार्ङ्गिणः
यस्याभूत् भुवनैश्चतुर्दशभिरप्यापूरणं दुर्लभम्

(sampūrṇam vidadhē gabhīramudaram
Raṅgēśituś śārṅgiṇaḥ,
yasyābhūt bhuvanais chaturdaśabhir api āpūraṇam
durlabham).[23]

Invocatory Verses

The bi-lingual copper-plate charters of the Pāṇḍyan kings, just like the Pallava records, begin with one or more invocatory verses in praise of various deities. In the Pāṇḍyan charters, we find many stanzas in praise of the Hindu Trinity, Brahma, Vishṇu and Śiva. However, unlike the Pallava inscriptions, there are no verses about Gaṇēśa or about any of the Goddesses like Lakshmī or Pārvatī.

Brahmā

In many of the Pāṇḍyan records like the Śrīvaramaṅgalam[24] and the Daḷavāypuram[25] copper-plates, the first among the Trinity, Lord Brahmā, the cause of the creation of the Universe, is praised in the invocatory verses.

The description of Brahmā, given by the poet of the Śrīvaramaṅgalam epigraph in the first verse in the *śārdūlavikṛīdita* metre, runs parallel to many of his descriptions given in the Purāṇas and other ancient texts. The verse of the Śrīvaramaṅgalam plates runs as follows:

'Hail! May that pure ancient sage (Brahmā), who resides in the primeval lotus, which has sprung out of the tank of Vishṇu's navel, who invokes with his four mouths, the sinless Brahman (i.e. the Vēda), which has revealed all sciences, and who bears a mass of matted hair, the colour of which is redder than the morning sun, maintain for a long time, your joy'.

ब्रह्मव्यञ्चितविश्वतन्त्रमनघं वक्त्रैश्चतुर्भिगृणन्
विभ्रद्बालपतङ्गपिङ्गलतरुच्छयाञ्चटामण्डलम् ।
आद्यन्नाभिसरः प्रसूति कमलं विष्णोरधिष्ठायकः
पुष्णातु प्रमदञ्चिराय भवतां पुण्यः पुराणो मुनिः ।।

(Brahma vyañchita viśvatantram anagham
vaktrais chaturbhir gṛiṇan,
bibhrat bāla pataṅga piṅgaḷa tarucchāyan chaṭāmaṇḍalam,
ādyānnābhisaraḥ prasūtikamalam Vishṇōr adhishṭāyakaḥ,
pushṇātu pramadan chirāya bhavatām puṇyah purāṇaḥ muniḥ).

Another verse found at the beginning of the Daḷavāypuram plates, extols Brahmā's position as a Creator, in *mandākrāntā* metre:

'May the lotus-born (Brahmā), whose form sprang from the husband of Lakshmī (i.e. Vishṇu), whose creations were the deities, the demons, the oceans and the seven worlds and whose face when cheerful, even to a little extent is capable of bestowing benefits like Indra's position, grant prosperity to you!'

लक्ष्मीनाथादभवदुदयो यस्य विश्वाधिनाथात्
यस्योत्पाद्यं ससुरदनुजाम्भोदयः सप्तलोकाः।
शाचीपत्य प्रभृतिफलदो यस्य सौमुख्यलेशो
भूयो भूयः कमलभवनो भूतये वः स भूयात्।।

(*Lakshmī-nāthād abhavad udayaḥ yasya viśvādhinātāt*
yasyotpādyam sa sura danujāmbhōdhayaḥ saptalōkāḥ
śāchīpatya prabhṛtiphalado yasya soumukhyalēśaḥ
bhūyōbhūyaḥ kamalabhavanaḥ bhūtayē vaḥ sa bhūyāt).

Vishṇu

The Śrīvaramaṅgalam[26], Daḷavāypuram[27], and the Smaller Siṉṉamaṉūr[28] copper-plate grants contain invocatory verses in praise of Lord Vishṇu. He is called by the poets of these charters by many of his names such as Tridhāma, Hari, and Purshōttama.

The Śrīvaramaṅgalam record opens with a beautiful and poetic description of Vishṇu:

'May that wonderful lusture (of Vishṇu) whose body consists of the Vēda, who rides on a bird, who destroys the *daityas* (asuras), whose splendour surpasses that of a new cloud (in blackness), who has lotus-eyes, from whom this universe springs at the beginning of the *yuga* and into whom it again enters at the end of the *yuga*, protect you'

यस्मादाविर्भवति परमाश्चर्य भूताद्युगादौ
यस्मिन्नेव प्रविशति पुनर्विश्वमेतद्युगान्ते
तद्वश्छन्दोमयतनुवयो वाहनन्दैत्यधातिः
ज्योतिः पातु द्युति जितनवाम्भोदमम्भोजनेत्रम्।।

(*yasmād āvirbhavati paramāścharya bhutād yugādhau*
yasminnēva praviśati punar viśvamētat yugāntē,
tad vaś chhandōmayatanu- vayōvāhanan daityaghātiḥ
jyōtiḥ pātu dyuti jita nava ambhōdam ambhōja-nētram)

The Daḷavāypuram plates also contain a very nice verse about this deity :

'May the brilliance of Vishṇu, who is understood by the Vēdāntas, whose form is inaccessible directly or by inference or by comparison or by intelligence, remove inauspiciousness'.

प्रत्यक्षानुमिति समत्व बोधक्लृप्ति ज्ञानानामविषय भूतरूपतत्त्वम्।
वेदान्तावगतमनादि मध्यहानि ज्योतिर्वोहरतु हरेर्मङ्गलानि।।

(pratyaksha-anumiti samatva bōdhaklipti
jñānānām avishaya bhūtarūpa-tatvam,
Vēdānta-avagatam anādhi madhyahāni
jyotiḥ vōharatu Harēḥ amaṅgaḷani)

Śiva

Likewise, the Sanskrit portions of the bi-lingual inscriptions of the Pāṇḍyas like the Vēḷvikuḍi,[29] Śrīvaramaṅgalam,[30] and Daḷavāypuram[31] plates begin with stanzas in praise of Śiva, who is called in these records by his names and epithets like Pinākin, Hara, etc.

A beautiful verse in the Vēḷvikuḍi charter, in praise of Śiva runs as follows, in *vrityanuprāsa alaṅkāru:*

'Hail! May Śiva, whose head ornament is the cool-rayed (moon), who is the (primeval) cause for the cessation of the sufferings of the devoted, who is beautiful with matted hair of golden hue, and who crushes the mischievous pride of Kandarpa (Cupid), grant you perpetual happiness'.

श्रियश्चिरं वश्शि शिरांशुशेखरश्शिवः
श्रितार्त्तिप्रतिवन्ध कारणं
तनो तु सौवर्ण कपर्द्दसुन्दरः
कुदर्प कन्दर्प मदप्रमर्द्दनः

(Śriyas chiram vaś śiśirāmśu śēkhara Śiva,
śritārthi pratibandha kāraṇam,
tanōtu sauvarṇa Kaparddha sundaraḥ,
kudarpa kandarpa mada pramarddhanaḥ)

The third verse in the Śrīvaramaṅgalam plates is about the greatness of the holy feet of Lord Śiva.

'May that pair of feet of Pinākin (Śiva) which removes all sins, by practicing devotion of which, perfect success is produced to men in this world and the next, and which appear to the lotuses (placed) as ornaments on the heads (which bear) glittering diadems of the Gods, protect you for a long time'.

अंहसंधति हारिणोरतिदृढं भक्तिं ययोः कुर्वतां
अत्रामुत्र च सम्भवन्त्यविकला सम्पन्तयो देहिनां
उत्तंसाम्बुरुह श्रियं कलयतो याषुत्तमाङ्गे लसन्
मौलौ नाकसदां पिनाकि चरणौ तौ वश्चिरं रक्षताम्।

(aṁha saṅghati hāriṇōr atidṛiḍam bhaktim yayōḥ kurvatām
atrāmutra cha saṁbhavantyavikalaḥ sampanttayoḥ dēhinām,
uttamsāṁbhuruha śriyam kalayataḥ yāśu uttamāṅge lassan
maulou nākasadām Pināki-charaṇou tou vaschiram rakshatām).

Echoes from Sanskrit Literature

In the copper-plate and lithic epigraphs of the Pāṇḍyan period also, we find a few instances where the poets of these records have reflected the ideas seen in a few works of Sanskrit literature, especially the poems of Kālidāsa like the *Raghuvaṁśa* and the *Mēghadūta*.

Sunandā's description of a Pāṇḍyan king in the *Raghuvaṁśa*:

'Agasthya, the controller of the great mountain Vindhyā, who completely drank up and again disgorged the ocean, is the person enquiring after the successful completion of the bath of this king whose body is wet with the bath after Aśvamēdha sacrifices'.

विन्ध्यस्य संस्तम्भयिता महाद्रेः
निश्शेषपीतोज्झित सिन्धुराजः।

प्रीत्याश्वमेधावमृथार्द्र मूर्तेः
सौस्नातिको यस्य भवत्यगस्त्यः।।

(Vindhyasya saṁstambhayitā mahādrēḥ
niśśesha pītōjjita-sindhurājaḥ,
prītyāśvamēdhou avabhrithārdra-mūrtēḥ
sousnātiko yasya bhavatyagastyaḥ).[32]

This is the model for a verse found in the Vēḷvikuḍi copper-plate grant of Neḍuñjaḍaiyaṉ:

'Victorious is the race of the Pāṇḍya kings, the mine of prosperity, whose family priest is the sage (Agastya), born of the pitcher, who stopped the rapidly growing (Vindhyā) mountain from (further) growth and drank all the water of the ocean'.

अस्तम्भयत्क्षितिधरं प्रविजृम्भमाणं
अम्भसमस्तमपिबज्जलधेश्च यस्य।
कुम्भोद्भवो भवति यस्य मुनिः पुरोधसा
श्रीनिधिर्जयति पाण्ड्य नरेन्द्र वंशः।।

(astambhayat kshiti-dharam pravijrimbhamāṇam
ambhasamastam apibajjaladhēścha yasya,
kuṁbhodbhavō bhavati yasya muniḥ purōdhasā-
śrīnidhir jayati Pāṇḍya narēndra vaṁśaḥ)[33]

Another verse in the *Raghuvaṁśa* is as follows:

'Formerly, the lord of Laṅkā, proudly desirous of conquering the kingdom of Indra, but apprehending attack in Janasthāna from this king (Pāṇḍya), who had obtained a powerful weapon from Śiva, concluded peace with him before starting out.'

अस्त्रं हरादाप्तवता दुरापं
येनेन्द्र लोकावजयाय दृप्तः।
पुरा जनस्थान विमर्दशङ्की
सन्धाय लङ्काधिपतिः प्रतस्थे।।

(astram Harād āptavatā durāpam
yēnēndra-lōkāvijayāya driptaḥ
purā Janasthāna vimarda śaṅkī
sandhāya Laṅkādhipatiḥ pratasthē).[34]

This has its echo in a line of the Larger Siṉṉamaṉūr plates of Rājasimha: 'another king whose commands could not be crossed made the ten-headed Rāvaṇa to ask for peace'

दशाननं सन्धि परञ्चकार
नरेश्वरः कश्चिदखण्डिताज्ञः

(daśānanam sandhiparam chakāra narēśvaraḥ kaschit akhaṇḍ-itājñaḥ).[35]

In the inscription of Jaṭāvarman Sundara Pāṇḍya engraved in the Raṅganāthasvāmi temple, Śrīraṅgam, we find a verse in which the poet of the record seems to have been influenced by a verse in the *Mēghadūta*:

'Reclining under the arch, which the sun among kings had made with masses of gold (taken) from the crowns of (his) enemies (and) which was adorned with numerous jewels, Hari, who dwells in the temple of Raṅga, surpasses a monsoon cloud which is surrounded by a rainbow.

कृतस्य नृप भास्वत रिपुकिरीट हैमोच्चयैः
अनेकमणि शोभिनो मकरतोरणस्यान्तरे।
हरिर्विरचितसिको जयति रंगधामाश्रय
पयोधर त्रिदशकार्मुकावेष्टितम्।।

(kṛitasya nṛipa-bhāsvata ripu-kirīṭa-haimōchchayaiḥ
anēka maṇi- śōbhinō makara-tōraṇasyāntarē,
Harir virachitāsikō jayati Raṅgadhāmāśraya
payōdhara-tridaśa kārmukāveshṭitam).[36]

In the above mentioned verse, the poet of this inscription appears to have taken the idea of Lord Raṅganātha looking like a monsoon cloud surrounded by a rainbow, from a verse of Kālidāsa's *Mēghadūta* but in an inverted way, since the latter work states that:

'the rain-bearing cloud with a rainbow in the background looks like Vishṇu in Kṛishṇāvatāra, black in complexion with a peacock's feather on his head

बर्हेणेव स्पुरित रुचिना गोपवेषस्य विष्णोः ।।
(*barhēṇēva spuritaruchinā gōpaveśasya Vishṇōḥ*).[37]

Metres of the Pāṇḍyan Inscriptions

1 *Āṇaimalai cave temple inscription of Varaguṇa* I (770 A.D) vv.1-2-Āryā, v.3-Vaṁśastha

2 *Smaller Siṉṉamaṉūr plates of Neḍuñjadaiyaṉ* (Varaguṇa I) vv.1-4-Anushṭubh

3 *Vēḷvikuḍi plates of Neḍuñjaḍaiyaṉ (Varaguṇa I)* (c. 770 A.D) vv. 1, 12 Vaṁśastha; vv. 2, 17, 20, 23 – Anushṭubh; vv. 3, 9, 19 – Vasantatilakā; vv. 4, 5, 6, 10 - Śārdūlavikrīḍitā; vv. 7, 8, 15, 16 – Mālabhariṇī; vv. 11, 14 – Upēndravajrā; v. 13 – Drutavilambitā; v.18 -Āryā

4 *Śrīvaramaṅgalam plates of Neḍuñjaḍaiyaṉ* (Varaguṇa I) (c. 785 A.D.)
vv. 1, 3, 5 - Śārdūlavikrīḍitā; vv. 2, 4 – Mandākrāntā; v. 6 - Śragdharā

5 *Daḷavāypuram plates of Parāntaka Vīranārāyaṇa* (c. 910 A.D.) vv. 1, 6, 7-Mandākrāntā; vv. 2, 9 – Praharśhiṇī; vv. 3, 11, - Vasantatilakā; vv.4, 5 Vaṁśastha; v.8-Drutavilaṁbita; vv. 10, 18, 34 - Śārdūlavikrīḍita; vv.12, 14, 36 – Upēndravajra; v.13 – Rathōddhata; vv.15, 21, 32 – Upajāti; vv.16, 17, 19, 20, 24, 31, 33, 35 - Indravajra; vv. 22, 23, 25-29, 37, 38, 40 - Anushṭubh; v.30 - Śragdharā; v.39 - Āryā

6 *Larger Siṉṉamaṉūr plates of Rājasiṁha II* (c. 926-927 A.D.) vv. 1 and 30 Upajāti; v. 2 – Vaiśvadēvī; vv. 3, 4, 5, 8, 31 – Upēndravajra; vv. 6, 7, 13, 27, 38 – Pushpitāgrā; vv. 9, 11, 14, 16, 23 - Śālinī; vv. 12 and 32 - Drutavilaṁbitā; vv. 15, 22, 26, 28, 29, 34, 36 Anushtubh; vv. 25, 33, 35 - Indravajrā;

v.24 – Mandākrāntā; vv. 10 & 20 - Śārdūlavikrīḍitā; v. 21 - Śragdharā; vv. 17, 18, 19, 37 – Vasantatilakā

7 *Śivakāśi plates of Vīra-Pāṇḍya* (c. 940-941 A.D) vv. 1, 4-6, 8, 9 – Indravajrā; vv.2, 3, 7, 11, 13-24, 27, 28 Anushṭubh; v.10 - Śragdhāra; vv. 12, 26 Śārdūlavikrīḍitā; v. 25 - Śālinī.

8 *Śrīraṅgam inscription of Jaṭāvarman Sundara Pāṇḍya* (13th century A.D.)
vv. 1, 7, 8, 10, 15, 20, 21, 23, 26, 29, 30- Śārdūlavikrīḍitā; v.11-Indravajra; vv.2,3,5,12,16,17,18,24,25,&27 Vasantatilakā; vv.4, 22 Mandākrāntā; vv.6, 13,14,19- Malinī; vv.9, 28-Pṛithvi

REFERENCES

1. *E.I.*, Vol. XVII, No.16, v.10, p.229 (Veḷvikuḍi copper-plate grant of Neḍuñjaḍaiyaṉ).
2. *E.I.*, Vol. III, No. 206, v. 8, p.451 (Larger Siṉṉamaṉūr plates of Rājasiṁha II).
3. *E.I.*, Vol. VIII, No. 33, pp. 319-20.
4. *E.I.*, Vol. XXXVI, No. 15, p.117.
5. Veḷvikuḍi plates, *op., cit.*, pp. 298-300.
6. *PCP*, pp. 56-57.
7. *DCVP*, pp. 13-31.
8. Larger Siṉṉamaṉūr plates, *op.cit.*, pp. 451-454.
9. *SCVP*, pp. 43-47.
10. *E.I.*, Vol. III, No. 2, pp.11-14.
11. Veḷvikuḍi plates, *op.cit.*, line 30, p. 300.
12. *DCVP*, v. 34, p. 18.
13. Larger Siṉṉamaṉūr plates, v. 38, p. 454.
14. *SCVP*, v. 26, pp. 46-47.
15. Veḷvikuḍi plates, *op.cit.*, v.12, p. 299.
16. *Ibid.*, v.16, pp. 299-300.
17. *DCVP*, v.16, p.15.
18. Larger Siṉṉamaṉūr plates, *op.cit.*, v. 13, p. 451.
19. *Ibid.*, v.18, p. 452.
20. *SCVP*, v. 8, p. 44.
21. *E.I.*, Vol. III, No. 2, v. 7, p. 12.
22. *Ibid.*, v. 20, p. 13.

23. *Ibid.*, v. 26, p. 14.
24. *PCP*, v.1, p. 56.
25. *DCVP*, v.1, p. 13.
26. *PCP*, v. 2, p. 56.
27. *DCVP*, v. 2, p. 13.
28. *S.I.I.*, Vol. III, No. 206, v. 1, p. 462 (Smaller Siṉṉamaṉūr plates).
29. Veḷvikuḍi plates, *op.cit.*, v. 1, p. 298.
30. *PCP*, v. 3, p. 56.
31. *DCVP*, v. 3, p.13.
32. Venkataraghavachariar, V., (Ed.) *Raghuvaṁśa Mahākāvya*, Madras, 1991, Sarga VI.61.
33. Veḷvikuḍi plates, *op.cit*, v. 3, p. 298; C. Sivaramamurti, *Epigraphical Echoes of Kāḷidāsa*, Madras, 1944, pp. 30-31.
34. *Raghuvaṁśa*, *op.cit.*, Sarga VI.62.
35. Larger Siṉṉamaṉūr plates, *op.cit.*, v.5, p. 451; C. Sivaramamurti, *op.cit.*, p. 31.
36. *E.I.*, Vol. III, No. 2, v. 9, p. 12.
37. Kale, M.R., *Mēghadūta* (text and translation), Delhi, 1991, *Pūrvamēgha*, v.15.

3

Chōḷa Period

The dynasty of the Imperial Chōḷas from the time of Vijayālaya (c. 850-871 A.D.) upto the time of Rājēndra III (1246-1279 A.D.), for about three and a quarter centuries have issued the largest number of epigraphs among all the dynasties of ancient Tamil Nadu. Compared to the period of the Pallava kings, the number of Sanskrit epigraphs of this period are comparatively lesser in number, since most of their records were composed in Tamil, the local language. However, there are many Chōḷa inscriptions, both lithic and copper-plate charters, which are composed wholly in Sanskrit or are bi-lingual like the Pallava and Pāṇḍyan ones.

The copper-plate grants of the Chōḷas are very important for this study as the Sanskrit introductory *praśasti* portions of these inscriptions are very long records, and consist of a lengthy string of verses in chaste and beautiful Sanskrit detailing the mythical genealogy of the Chōḷa-vaṁśa, and then the line of historical personages and their various achievements upto the period of the ruler in whose reign the record was composed.

The bi-lingual copper-plate charters which have been

discovered till now and on which special attention will be focussed in this chapter are the Vēḷāñjēri plates of Parāntaka I (c. 932 A.D.),[1] the Anbil plates of Parāntaka II (Sundara Chōḷa) (961 A.D.),[2] the Larger Leiden plates of Rājarāja I (1006 A.D),[3] the Tiruvālaṅgāḍu plates (1018 A.D.),[4] Karandai plates (1021 A.D.),[5] and the Eśālam plates[6] of Rājēndra I. The bi-lingual Karandai plates deserve special mention as it is the biggest copper-plate grant discovered so far, consisting of fifty-seven plates and weighing 111.73 kilograms.

The Tiruvālaṅgāḍu plates, also a very lengthy document, consists of thirty-one copper sheets and weighs 93.05 kilograms, but the Sanskrit *praśasti* section of this record is much longer than that found in the Karandai epigraph.

The other copper-plate documents, namely, the Vēḷāñjēri, Anbil, Larger Leiden and Eśālam records are comparatively smaller, but are very important for the study of the literary beauty of the Sanskrit verses contained therein.

Among the lithic inscriptions of the Chōḷa period, although there are a very large number of small Sanskrit inscriptions found on the walls of the temples, they are not of any special interest for this study as they do not have much by way of literary merit in them. However, there are a few long stone epigraphs of this period which deserve special mention. Among the lithic records which have been analyzed in-depth in this chapter, one of the most important ones is the Kanyākumarī inscription of Vīra-Rājēndra (1069 A.D), found inscribed on six pillars in the *maṇi-maṇḍapa* of the Kanyā-Bhagavatī temple at Kanyākumarī in the southern-most tip of Tamil Nadu.[7] This inscription, a *'Chōḷa-vaṁśa-praśasti'* is composed mostly in Sanskrit verse and has only a small Tamil section following it. The large Sanskrit section consists of eighty-one verses, and is one of the longest Sanskrit lithic inscriptions of Tamil Nadu. It is very interesting to note that the Sanskrit section of this inscription is exactly the same, verse for verse, as the Chārāla copper-plate grant of the same king (1069 A.D.) discovered in Chitoor district, Andhra Pradesh.[8]

The other important lithic records of this period are the inscriptions of a general named Naralōkavīra of the Chōḷa ruler, Kulōttuṅga I (1071-1122 A.D), found at places like the Naṭarāja temple at Chidambaram,[9] the Varadarājasvāmi temple, Kāñchīpuram[10] and at Siddhaliṅgamaḍam (South Arcot district).[11]

All the Sanskrit inscriptions mentioned above were issued at the time of a grant of land or money to temples and to the learned and holy *brāhmaṇas* of the land. The Chōḷa rulers, like their predecessors, the Pallava and Pāṇḍya monarchs were well-versed in the sacred lore. Rājēndra I is described in the Karandai copper-plates as being well-versed in all the Vēdas and Śāstras (*akhila-vēda-śāstra-vit*).[12] He also held the title *Paṇḍita Chōḷa*[13] while Rājarāja III was called *Rāja Paṇḍita*.[14] These rulers, therefore continued the tradition of the Tamil kings before them and gave a great fillip to Sanskrit learning and literature.

Poets of the Choḷa Inscriptions

Like the Sanskrit inscriptions of the Pallavas, the epigraphs of the Chōḷa dynasty were also composed by many poets and some of these inscriptions mention the names of these composers at the very end of the records.

Among the copper-plate records of the Chōḷa period, the earliest of these, the Vēḷāñjēri plates of Parāntaka Chōḷa I, records that the Sanskrit verses were composed by a person named Rutsa.[15] Unfortunately, no other details about this poet are available from this inscription as some portions of this epigraph are damaged.

Another Sanskrit epigraph of the period of the same king, the Shōḷingūr Rock inscription, records in the concluding portion, that this *praśasti* was composed by the sage Kumāra, belonging to the Kāśyapa *gōtra* and the *Vaikhānasa sūtra.*[16]

The Anbil copper-plate charter of Parāntaka II or Sundara Chōḷa written in 961 A.D., records that the Sanskrit *praśasti* of this epigraph was composed by a poet named Mādhava-Bhaṭṭa *yajvan*. In the very last verse of this inscription, he describes himself and his family in a very poetic manner thus:

'Of Bhaṭṭa-Daṭṭa, who was an ocean for the rivers of learning, a mine of the most spotless good qualities, a moon to the ocean which was the family of Parāśara and a bee at the lotus-like feet of the consort of Lakshmī (Vishṇu), the son, Mādhava-Bhaṭṭa *yajvan*, composed this *praśasti* bedecked with various meanings.'

विद्यानद्यंबुराशिर्विमलतरगुणव्रातरत्नाकरो यः
पाराशर्यान्वयाम्बुधिशिशिरकरो भट्टदत्ताभिधानः।
तस्य श्रीनाथ पादाम्बुरुहयुगलिका षट्पदस्य प्रशस्तिम्
पुत्रश्चित्रार्थरम्यां समचरयदिमां माधवो भट्टयज्वा।।

(*vidyā-nadhyaṁbu-rāśir-vimalataraguṇa vrātaratnākaro yaḥ*
pārāśaryānvayambudhi-śiśirakaro Bhaṭṭā-daṭṭābhidhānaḥ,
tasya Śrīnātha pādāmburuhayugaḷikā-shaḍpadasya praśastim,
putraś chitrārtha-ramyām samarachayad imām
Mādhavō Bhaṭṭa yajvā).[17]

Among the other Chōḷa copper-plate inscriptions, the Tiruvālaṅgāḍu, Karandai and Eśālam epigraphs were composed during the reign of Rājēndra Chōḷa I (1012-1044 A.D.). With regard to the Larger Leiden plates, while the Tamil portion of this record was written in the reign of Rājarāja Chōḷa I (985-1014 A.D.), the Sanskrit *praśasti* portion, was added on to the original Tamil section during the period of his son and successor, Rājēndra Chōḷa I.[18] One of the last few verses of the Sanskrit section of the Larger Leiden plates mentions that the composer of this *praśasti* was

Anantanārāyaṇa, who belonged to the village of Kōṭṭaiyūr and was born in the Vasishṭha *gōtra*.

ग्रामे रम्ये जगति महिते कोठ्ठयूरभिधाने
लक्ष्मीधामनि अजनि विमले यः वसिष्ठान्ववाये।
सत्संसेवि विमलचरितः अनन्तनारायणाख्यः
सोयं धीमानरचयदिमां अग्रजन्मा पशस्तिम्।।

(grāmē ramyē jagati mahitē Kōṭṭaiyūr-abhidhānē
Lakshmī-dhāmani ajani vimalē yo Vasishṭhānvavāyē,
sat saṁsēvi vimala charito Anantanārāyaṇākhyaḥ
sōyam dhīman arachayadimām agrajanma praśastim).[19]

The Tiruvālaṅgāḍu plates record that the learned poet Nārāyaṇa, son of Śaṅkara and a devotee of the enemy of (the demon) Mura (i.e.) Vishṇu, composed this grant.

शंकरस्य सुतेनेदं भक्तेन मुरविद्द्विषः।
नारायणेन कविना शासनं कृतिना कृतम्।।

(Śaṅkarasya sutēnēdam bhaktēna muraviddvishaḥ,
Nārāyaṇēna kavinā śāsanam kṛitinā kṛitam).[20]

The Karandai copper-plate record, likewise states that the *praśasti* of this inscription was composed by the poet Nārāyaṇa, son of Śaṅkarārya and a resident of Pārśva-grāma or the neighbouring village.

शंकरार्यात्मजेनेदं पार्श्वग्रामनिवासिना
नारायणेन कविना शासनं शाश्वतं कृतम्।।

(Śaṅkarāryātmajēna idam Pārśva-grāma nivāsina,
Nārāyaṇēna kavinā śāsanam śāśvatam kṛitam).[21]

Again, the Eśālam record mentions the very same facts as the Karandai record thus:

शंकरस्य तनुजेन पार्श्वग्राम निवासिना
नारायणेन कविना शासनं शाश्वतं कृतम्।।

(Śaṅkarasya tanūjēna Pārśvagrāma-nivāsinā,
Nārāyaṇēna kavina śāsanam śāśvatam kṛitam)[22].

According to K.G. Krishnan, the Sanskrit sections of the Tiruvālaṅgāḍu and the Karandai plates were composed by one and the same poet Nārāyaṇa, who is identical with Anantanārāyaṇa of the Larger Leiden plates.[23] The Eśālam plates were also composed by this very same poet.[24]

It is likely that this talented composer was the court-poet of Rājēndra Chōḷa I. There are 137 verses in the Tiruvālaṅgāḍu plates, 76 verses in the Karandai plates, 48 verses in the Larger Leiden plates and 35 verses in the Eśālam copper-plates. According to P. Radhakrishna Sarma, it is quite natural that the first of these four *praśastis* which describe the same pedigree of a king might be an elaborate one, while the other ones were gradually reduced to avoid repetition and monotony, without omitting persons and events of political importance, of course, mentioning new ones if necessary and adding new verses of exquisite poetic beauty and changing the words, sentences and metres to give freshness to ideas and events already described.[25]

The long lithic inscription of Vīra-Rājēndra (1062/63-1070 A.D.), a son and successor of Rājēndra I found inscribed in the temple of Goddess Kanyākumarī in the town of Kanyākumarī[26] consists of 81 beautiful verses, but unfortunately this epigraph does not contain the name of the scholarly and talented poet who composed it. However, another inscription, a bi-lingual copper-plate grant, of the period of the same king discovered in Chārāla village (Chitoor district, Andhra Pradesh) was found to be identical, verse for verse with the Kanyākumarī inscription, but also contains a few more Sanskrit verses in addition to those found in the Kanyākumarī grant in a section which follows the Tamil portion. In these last few verses, the name of the poet is mentioned as Chandrabhūshaṇa Bhaṭṭa, the verse stating clearly that:

'this (panegreic) illuminating the prowess of Vīra-

Rājēndradēva was composed by the pure-minded Chandrabhūshaṇa Bhaṭṭa'

वीरराजेन्द्रदेवस्य विक्रमस्य प्रकाशनम्।
चन्द्रभूषण भट्टेन रचितं शुद्धबुद्धिना।।

(Vīrarājēndradēvasya vikramasya prakāśanam,
Chandrabhūshaṇa Bhaṭṭēna rachitam suddha-buddhina).[27]

A few verses later in the Chārāla plates this same poet is referred to by the paraphrased name Śaśibhūshaṇa-Paṇḍita.[28]

With regard to the many of the other lengthy Sanskrit lithic inscriptions of the Chōḷa period, such as the one at Chidambaram describing the benefactions of the general Naralōkavīra,[29] it is indeed sad that they do not include the names of the poets who composed them.

On the other hand, it is very interesting to note that some of the very short stone inscriptions, consisting of not more than one or at the most two verses, contain the name of the composer. For example, a record of the period of Kulōttuṅga Chōḷa I (1071-1122 A.D), found in the Vyāgrapādēśvara temple in Siddhaliṅgamaḍam (South Arcot district), consisting of only one verse recording the construction of this temple, mentions that the composer's name was Āṇḍapiḷḷai-bhaṭṭan.[30]

Literary Beauty of the Choḷa Inscriptions

The *praśastis* of the bi-lingual copper-plate inscriptions of the Chōḷas as well as a few of the lithic inscriptions of this dynasty mentioned earlier, are replete with poetic beauty, composed as they are in various *alaṅkāras* and metres. In the following pages, some of the beautiful verses from these records have been highlighted.

Verse twelve of the Vēḷāñjēri plates of Parāntaka I, composed in *vasantatilakā* metre by poet Rutsa, extolls the birth of his patron-king to Āditya I beautifully, using the *tulyayōgita alaṅkāra*, as follows:

'Just as the moon emanated from the milky-ocean, as the waters of the Gaṅgā from the Himālayas, as the heat-energy from the sun and as the Trikūta from Mount Mēru, so also Parāntaka was born of him'.

क्षीरार्णवादिव शशीतुहिनाचलेन्द्रात्
गंगाप्रवाहः इव भानुरिवोष्णभावः।
मेरोरिवाचलपतेः महितः त्रिकूटतः
तस्मादजायत परान्तक नामधेयः।।

(Kshirārṇavādiva śasi tuhināchalēndrāt
Gaṅgā-pravāhaḥ iva bhānurivoshṇabhāvaḥ
Mērōrivāchalapatēḥ mahitaḥ trikūtataḥ
tasmāt ajāyata Parāntaka nāmadēyaḥ)[31]

The very next verse is a perfect example of *ullēkha alaṅkāra* and is again a description of Parāntaka I, where the poet describes how different people view him in different relationships:

'The opponent kings considered him as death incarnate, wise men as Bṛihaspati, beloveds as *chintāmaṇi* (wishing stone), the subjects held him as their parent; good people as a treasure house; and damsels as the lord of love (Manmata himself).

मृत्युं रिपुक्षितिभृतः धिषणं बुधेन्द्राः
चिन्तामणिं प्रणयिनः पितरं प्रजाश्च।
सन्तस्स्वयं गृहनिधिं सभनस्वदेहं
यन्मन्वते मकरकेतुं अधीरनेत्राः।।

(mṛityum ripu-kshiti-britaḥ, dhishaṇam bhudēndrāḥ,
chintāmaṇim praṇayinaḥ pitaram prajāscha,
santas svayam gṛihanidhim, sabhana svadēham
yanmanvatē makara-kētum adhīra-nētrāḥ). [32]

The Anbil plates of Parāntaka II or Sundara Chōḷa (961 A.D.), consisting of forty-six verses in as many as seventeen different metres, is another beautiful poem. While describing king Sundara Chōḷa, the poet uses *rūpaka alaṅkāra* along with *ślēsha* to enhance the beauty of the comparison of the king with the sun:

'This king, by his feet (that are the rays), coming into contact with the tops of multitude of crests of kings (which are the mountains); by making the complete circle of the whole earth deeply attached (1) attachment (2) red colour), by dispelling on all sides the ignorance (which is the mass of darkness), by his eminent renown (which is the light) reaching all the quarters and being the sole cause of delight of Lakshmī (which is the lotus flower), displayed immediately after he was born, the splendour of the newly risen sun.'

उदयन्नेवावनिभृन्मकुटतटघटाकोटिलीढांघ्रिपीठः
कुर्वाणो रक्तरक्तं वलयमविकलं विश्वविश्वंभरायाः।
पद्मानन्देकहेतुः परिविधिततमोराशिराशावकाश
प्राप्तोदग्र प्रकाश श्रियमभितनुते यश्च बालहिमांशो।।

(udyannēva avani-bhṛin makuṭa-taṭa-ghaṭa koṭi-līḍāngri-pīṭhaḥ
kurvāṇō raktaraktam valayam avikalam viśva viśvaṁbharāyāḥ,
padmānandēkahētuḥ parividhitatamōrāśirāśāvakāśa
prāptōdagra prakāśa śrīyam abhitanutē yaḥscha bālāhimāmśōḥ).[33]

In the same Anbil plates, while describing an ancestor Vīra Chōḷa we come across the beauty of expression rather than the idea:

'In him valour had its goal, skill was incarnate, courage had a steady hold, goodness found a protector, the earth had a good king, poetic art a proper seat, skill in the fine arts found a common shelter and his fame caused astonishment in all quarters'.

शौर्यं सावधि रूपिणी चतुरता सालंवना धीरता
सौजन्यञ्च सनाथतामुपगतं राजन्वती मेदिनी।
सस्थाना कविता कलाकुशलता जाता समेताश्रया
यस्मिन्विस्मय नीयतामुपगता कीर्तिदिगन्तेष्वभूत्।।

śōuryam sāvadhi rūpiṇī chaturatā sālambanā dhīratā
soujañyañcha sanāthathāmupagatam rājanvatī mēdinī
sastānā kavitā kalā kuśalatā jātā samētāśrayā
yasmin vismaya nīyatāmupagatā kīrtirdigantēśhvabhūt.[34]

In verse 30 of the same plates while describing the marching of the army the poet gives us the beauty of idea using *sandēha alaṅkāra:*

'The dust raised by the army of the king leads the multitude of Gods dwelling in the heavens to conjecture thus:

'Is it that the circular world has reached the sky through a desire to have a look at the heaven? Or else the supporter of the world wishing to create a world spreads the cloud of dust? Or is it the smoke of the spreading fire to the destruction of the world'?

पृथ्वोश्चक्रं किमेतद् गगनमुपगतं स्वर्दिदृक्षाभिनूनं
किं वा लोकान् सिसृक्षोस्सपदि च रजसा त्रायते लोकभर्तुः।
आहोस्विल्लोक भंगप्रसृत हुतवहोद्धूत धूमप्रपञ्चः
स्वस्थैरेवं वितर्क्यो भवति सुरगणै र्यस्य सेनापरागः।।

pṛitvōschakram kimētad gaganamupagatam
sva didrikshā-bhinūnam,
kim va lōkān sisrikshōssapadi cha rajasā trāyatē lōkabhartuḥ,
āhōsvillōka–bhangaprasrita-hutavahōdbhūta-dhūma-
prapañchaḥ,
svasthairēvam vitarkyō bhavati suraganair-yasya sēnāparāgaḥ.[35]

Anantanārāyaṇa (Nārāyaṇa), composer of the Sanskrit *praśasti* of the Larger Leiden plates, consisting of forty-eight verses in various metres, handles the subject of death in a very poetic manner. While describing the passing away of Rājāditya, the crown-prince and son of Parāntaka I, he states 'that he went to give pleasure to the lotus faces of the heavenly damsels.'

राजादित्ये सुरपुरवधूवक्त्रपंकेरुहाणां प्रीतिं कर्तुं गतवति

(*Rājadityē surapura-vadhū-vaktra-pankēruhāṇām*
prītim karttum gatavati).[36]

In the very next verse, he describes the death of Rājaditya's younger brother, Gaṇḍarāditya thus:

' Gandarāditiya went to heaven for achieving the objects of the other world'

निजेन नाम्नात्रहेतोः स दिवं जगाम
(*nijēna nāmnātrahētōḥ sa divam jagāma*).[37]

About the death of Parāntaka II (Sundara Chōḷa), this poet says that:

'he directed his attention to protect the world of the gods'

सुरलोक परित्राण परे तस्मिन् परान्तके
(*suralōka paritrāṇa parē tasmin Parāntakē*).[38]

The same poet composed the Tiruvāḷaṅgāḍu copper-plate grant of Rājēndra I in twenty-one metres. While mentioning the mythological ancestors of the line of the Chōḷas, he describes king Sāṁkṛiti in a verse in *svagata* metre which also carries two meanings, as one 'who highly reddened (i.e. pleased) the earth with the (white) rays of the moon of (his) fame which is (indeed) strange'.

यः यशश्शशिमरीचिभिरुच्चैः अन्वरञ्जयदिलां इति चित्रम्।
(*yaḥ yaśaśśaśīmarīchibhirucchaiḥ
anvarañjayad ilām iti chitram*).[39]

While describing another ancestral king, Aryamā by name we come across a beautiful statement:

'Aryamā obtained Lakshmī (victory) by stirring the ocean of his enemy forces with the churning rod of his mountain-like arm'.

अर्यमा निजभुजाचलमन्थक्षोभितार जलधेर्हृत लक्ष्मीः
*Aryamā nijabhujāchala-mantha-kshōbhitāra-jaladhēr
hṛita lakshmīḥ.*[40]

Yet another ancestor whose name was Vallabha, 'offered his enemies as moths to the flames of his arrows'

सायकाग्नि शलभीकृत शत्रुर्यश्चकार
sāyakāgni-śalabhīkṛita śatruryaschakāra.[41]

In a verse in *svāgata* metre, the hatred that king Parāntaka I bore towards his enemies is described thus: 'the fire of whose anger after burning his enemies, was quenched not in the waters of the sea, (but), subsided (only) by the tears of the wives of the Siṁhaḷa (king) who was cut to pieces by his weapons'.

यस्य कोपदहनो दहनद्विषश्शान्तिमाप न समुद्रवारिणि।
शस्त्रकृत्तहतसिंहलांगना नेत्रवारिणि समञ्जगाम च।।
(*yasya kōpa-dahanō dahan dvishaśśāntimāpa na samudra vāriṇī, śastra-kṛita hata Simhaḷānganā netravāriṇī samañjagāna cha*).[42]

The composer of this charter describes the birth of Aruḷmōḷivarman (later coronated as Rājarāja I) in a very poetic way:

'The Nāga women danced on the occasion of the birth of this emperor, saying this (king), in all probability shall relieve our husband (i.e., Ādiśēsha) of the weight of the earth on his head'

भर्त्तृभूभरमसौ विनेष्यति प्रायशो न इति नागयोषितः।
कुर्वते च परिनर्तनन्दता जन्मलब्धौ इति चक्रवर्तिनि।।
(*bhartri bhū-bharam asau vinēśyati prāyaśo na iti nāga-yōshitaḥ,*
kurvatē sma parinārtananandatā janma labdou iti chakravartini).[43]

Just as poet Nārāyaṇa described the passing away of the kings of the Chōḷa dynasty in a poetic manner in the Larger Leiden inscription, in the Tiruvālaṅgāḍu epigraph also, he puts to use all his powers of imagination to describe similar incidents in a very poetic way. About the death of Sundara Chōḷa, this composer says,:

'King Sundara Chōḷa of great prowess, went to heaven, requested (as it were) by the assemblage of Gods to protect (it) immediately from the attack of the armies of demons and demi-gods'.

रक्षितुं क्षितिपतिस्सुरलोकं दैत्यदानववलैरुपरुद्धम्।
प्रार्थितस्सुरगणैरतिसूरः प्राप्तवान् सपदि सुन्दर चोलः।।

(rakshitum kshiti-patis sura-lōkam
daitya-dānava-balair uparuddham,
prārthitas sura-gaṇair atisūraḥ
prāptavān sapadi Sundara Chōḷaḥ).[44]

In the very next verse, the composer describes the act of *sati* by Sundara-Chōḷa's queen, Vānavaṉmahādēvī, on the death of her husband:

'I am determined to follow my lord Sundara (i.e., the beautiful), before (he) is coveted by celestial damsels', so saying zealously, his devoted queen the glorious Vānavaṉmahādēvī, like Arundhatī, in (her) manifold good qualities, abandoned her own people and followed him as (night) the day, to heaven, afraid as it were, of the allurement (of her husband) by celestial nymphs and (desirous consequently of) being near him even there.'

देवस्त्रीभिरलोभितो भवति मे यावत्पतिस्सुन्दरः
तावद्गन्तुमहं प्रवृत्तमतिरित्याख्यातवत्यादरात्
सार्द्धं तेन गता निशादिनमिव त्यकत्वा स्वकीयञ्जनम्
देवी तस्य पतिव्रता गुणगणैस्साक्षादरुन्धत्यसौ।

(dēvastrībhiralōbhito bhavati mē yāvat patisSundaraḥ)
tāvad gantum aham pravṛitta matir ityākhyātavatyādarāt
sārddham tēna gatā niśā dinamivā tyaktvā svakīyam janam
dēvī tasya pativratā guṇagaṇaiśsākshāt Arundatyasou).[45]

A few stanzas later, the death of Āditya (Karikāla), the son of Sundara Chōḷa is stated by the poet, punning on the word Āditya meaning sun:

'Āditya, disappeared (from this world) with a desire to see heaven'.

गतवान् अस्तं आदित्यः स्वर्दिदृक्षया।

(gatavān astam Ādityaḥ svardidrikshaya).[46]

In the same inscription, the composer mentions the practice of conducting the *tulābhāra* ceremony which was performed frequently by the rulers of the Chōḷa dynasty. Here, the poet talks about the *tulābhāra* of Rājarāja I in *arthāntaranyāsya* in *anushṭubh* metre:

' Although in the *tulābhāra* (ceremony), the king was weighed against gold-pieces in the scales (*tula*), he was still (found) *a-tula* (i.e., unequalled). (Hence), it is difficult to comprehend the greatness of the great'

तुलितोऽपि तुलाभारे तुलया हेमभिर्नृपः
सोऽतुलोभूत् अविज्ञेयो महिमा महतामतः
(*tulitōpi tulābhārē tulayā hēmabhirnṛipaḥ,*
so atulōbhūt avijñēyo mahimā mahatām ataḥ).[47]

The Chālukyas of Kalyāṇi and the Chōḷas were sworn enemies and their wars have been frequently referred to in the Sanskrit *praśastis* of the Chōḷa epigraphs. The founder of the Chālukyan dynasty was Taila and the poet of the Tiruvālaṅgādu charter often uses the name of this king (*taila* means oil in Sanskrit) to beautify his verses, where descriptions of battles between the two armies occur, for example between Chālukya Satyāśraya and Rājarāja Chōḷa I (Aruḷmo-ḷivarman) and again between Satyāśraya's descendent Jayasiṁha and Rājarāja's son Rājēndra Chōḷa I.

'This is strange, that though Satyāśraya fled to avoid misery from the attack of his (i.e. Aruḷmoḻivarman's) ocean-like army, (still) misery found a (permanent) abode in him. But this is not strange, that his flight is due to (i.e. the result of his) birth from Taila'

सत्याश्रयो यद्बलसिन्धुरोधात् कष्टं परित्यज्य पलायितोपि।
कष्टाश्रयश्चित्रमिदं न चित्रं तैलप्रभावात् द्रवणं यदस्य।।
(*Satyāśrayō yadbalasindhu-rōdhāt kashṭam parityajya palāyitōpi,*
kashtāśrayaśchitram idam na chitram taila-prabhāvāt dravaṇam yadasya).[48]

In verse 101, which is a fine example of *Vibhāvana alaṅkāra*, the poet states about Rājēndra I,

'It may be no wonder that the fire of his anger, burst into a flame as it came into contact with the descendent of Taila, but it is strange that the fire of his anger consumed the fuel (Taila) having crossed the great waters of the ocean'.

तैलस्य सन्ततिमवाप्य तदीयकोपवह्निस्समुज्वलितवानिति नैव चित्रम्।
चित्रन्त्विदं भवति सर्वसमुद्रवारीण्युल्लङ्य यन्निरदहद्विषनिन्दनानि।।

tailasya santatim avāpya tadīya kōpa-vahni
samujvalitavāniti naiva chitram
chitramtvidam bhavati sarva-samudra-
vārīnyullangya yanniradahadvishadindanani.[49]

A beautiful but poignant description of the widowed queens of Jayasiṁha, the Chālukyan enemy of Rājēndra I is given by poet Nārāyaṇa with great poetic beauty in *Indravajra* metre in *Virōdhabhasa alaṅkara:*

'While this king with anger was engaged in vanquishing Jayasiṁha, very strangely, the fire of grief of the Raṭṭa ladies burst into flame, washed by the tears (trickling) from (their) eyes'

तस्मिन् समुद्योगवति क्षितीशे जेतुंसकोपे जयसिंहराजम्।
रट्टाङ्गनानां नयनाम्बुसिक्तश्शोकाग्निराशि र्ज्वलितोति चित्रम्।।

(*tasmin samudyōgavati kshitīśē jētum sakōpe Jayasiṁharājam,*
Raṭṭāṅganānām nayanāmbusikta śōkāgnirāśīr jvalitoti chitram).[50]

This is followed by another verse on the same theme which is effectively portrayed here in *virōdhābhāsa alaṅkāra* in *vasantatilakā* metre in which the poet states that:

'Although these queens being widows stood bereft of ornaments, yet they looked as brilliant and beautiful as before with shining pearls, because of their drops of tears'.

तच्चण्ड् दण्ड परिखण्डित रट्टराज नारी पयोधरतटान्यविभूषणानि।
तन्नेत्रवारिकणिकोज्वलमौक्तिकानि तत्कान्तिमन्ति विलसन्ति महान्यभूवन्।।

(tachchaṇḍa-daṇḍa-parikaṇḍita-Raṭṭarāja-nāri payōdhara-taṭāny avibhūshaṇāni tannētra-varikaṇikōjvala-mauktikāni tat kāntimanti vilasanti mahānyabhūvan).[51]

The poet also refers to Rājēndra's victory over king Indraratha of the Lunar race (the race descended from the moon) thus in *pushpitāgra* metre:

'The white parasol of that king, the jewel of the lunar race, fell (to the ground) its (supporting) staff and the top being cut (asunder) in battle by sharp arrows, as if the disc of the moon (fell), distressed by the defeat (of her descendent)'.

निशितशरनिकृत्तदण्डमस्तं युधिधवलातप वारणं पपात।
शशिकुलतिलकस्य तस्य राज्ञः परिभवखिन्नतयेव चन्द्रबिंबम्।

(niśita-śara-nikṛita-daṇḍamastam yudhi dhavaḷātapa vāraṇam papāta, śaśi-kula-tilakasya tasya rajñaḥ paribhavakhinnatayeva chandra-bimbam).[52]

The bi-lingual Karandai copper-plate grant, the largest of all such inscriptions discovered so far, is also of the period of Rājēndra Chōḷa, and poet Nārāyaṇa, the composer of the other inscriptions seen so far was also the composer of the Sanskrit portion of this charter. This *praśasti* portion contains seventy-six verses, and is smaller than that of the Tiruvālaṅgāḍu plates. However, the Karandai plates contain beauty of ideas and some of the more interesting verses which reflect this poet's imagination and skill with words are given below.

In verse thirty-four of this record, the poet describes the heroism of Rājarāja I and his victory over Satyāśraya, the Chālukyan king in *śārdūlavikrīḍita* metre:

'He, with his arms (resembling) the Mandara mountain, rapidly and energetically churned the ocean of Satyāśraya's armies, that had covered the whole earth, and that had its rows of horses, resembling the eddying waves, the crowds of elephants resembling the crocodiles, the multitudes of foot-soldiers resembling the masses of waters and quickly seized the moon of fame along with the Lakshmī of victory'.

अश्वश्रेणि परंपरोर्मिवलयं मातङ्गनक्राकुलं
पट्टिव्रातविलोलवारिनिकरं प्रच्छन्नभूमण्डलं।
आदत्तासु जयश्रियं सहयशस् चन्द्रेण सत्याश्रय
आनीकाद्धिं भुजमन्दरेण तरसा निर्मात्यवेगेन यः।।

(aśva-śrēṇi paramparōrmi-valayam mātaṅga-nakrākulam
pattivrāta vilōlavāri-nikaram prachchhanna bhūmaṇḍalam,
ādhattāśu jayaśriyam saḥ yaśas chandrēṇa Satyāśraya
ānīkadhvi bhuja-mandarēṇa tarasā nirmātya vēghēna yaḥ).[53]

A few verses later, the composer, using his poetic imagination, while describing Rājarāja's conquest of the various directions states :

'the glory of Indra, Yama, Varuṇa and Kubēra was taken away by the king, one after another, the foremost among men, after having conquered their quarters'.

संपत् सुरेन्द्रस्य यमस्य चापि
प्राचेतसो वैश्रवणस्य या या।
सासा हृतासीत् नृपवरेण तेन
क्रमेण जित्वा हरितस्सदीयः।।

(sampat surēndrasya yamasya chāpi,
prāchētasō vaiśravaṇasya yāyā
sāsā hṛitāsīt nṛipavarēṇa tēna,
kramēṇa jitva haritaḥ tadīyaḥ).[54]

While referring to the infanthood of Rājēndra Chōḷa I, this poet describes the simple act of this child learning to walk with the help of his mother in a very beautiful and poetic style thus:

'Holding his foster mother's hands with his, he placed

his steps slowly on the earth, as if doubting whether the earth will be capable of bearing his weight or not'.

शनैश्शनैर्भूमितले पदानि न्यदत्त धात्रीकर संगिहस्तः।
सोढुं किमीष्टे गरिमाणं उर्वी न वा मां इत्येव संशयानः।।

(śanaiśśanair bhūmitalē padāni nyadatta dhātrīkara-saṅgi-hastaḥ, sōḍum kimīshṭē garimāṇam ūrvi na vā mām ityēva samśayānaḥ).[55]

The poet of this charter, in one of the last few verses of the Karandai inscription glorifies his king Rājēndra I using methophors (*rūpaka*) thus:

'He was a pond for the playing of the swan of learning; a wide playground for Lakshmī of logic; the birthplace of courage, intellect, love, wealth and compassion; a touchstone for assessing the paṇḍits of the learned assembly; a lamp of learning into the hidden truths of the concourse of *śrutis*, known and unknown'.

विद्याहंसी विहरणसरो वादलक्ष्मी विशाल
क्रीडास्थानं धृतिमतिरतिश्रीदया जनमभूमिः।
विद्वदगोष्ट्यां निकषणशिला पण्डितानां प्रमात्रि
दृष्टादृष्ट श्रुतिपतगुहा तत्वविज्ञान दीपः।।

(vidyāhamsī-viharaṇa-sarō vāddha-Lakshmī-viśāla krīdā-sthānam, driti-mati-rati-śrī-dayā-janma-bhūmiḥ, vidvad gōshṭhyām nikashaṇa-śilā paṇḍitānām pramātri, drishtā-drishṭa-śruti-patha-guhā-tatva-vijñāna-dīpaḥ).[56]

The above-mentioned verse is almost the same as a stanza found in the Eśālam plates of the same ruler, also composed by the same poet and which is the smallest of the Sanskrit *praśasti* sections among all the Chōḷa copper-plate grants.[57]

The Kanyākumarī lithic inscription of Vīra-Rājēndra, which contains one of the longest Sanskrit *praśastis* among the Chōḷa epigraphs, also has some very beautiful verses of poetic beauty. Verse two of this inscription is in praise of Śiva and verse three is in praise of Vishṇu. Verse two reads as follows:

'May the God Śaṁbhu, who is merciful to all objects, animate and inanimate, who, in his resplendent body, poised in attitude on the (Kailāsa) mountain, successfully carries this supreme Māya, which makes this world pleasant and is the cause of knowledge and ignorance; who, being pleased with the happiness enjoyed by all creatures (*paśus*), protect you from falling, in order that your connection with sin may easily break asunder'.

माया मायामिनीं यो वहति जगदिदं रञ्जयन्तीं जयन्तीं
ज्ञानाज्ञान प्रसूति स्फुटरुचिवपुषा योगभाजागभाजा।
सत्वासत्वानुकम्पी हितमुदित महातापशूनां पशूनां
शम्भुनम्भुग्न पापव्यति कृति भवतस्सप्रपानात् प्रपातात्।।

(māyā māyaminīm yō vahati jagat idam rañjayantīm jayantīm,
jñānājñāna prasūti sphuṭa ruchi vapushā yōgabhājāga bhūjā,
satvāsatvānukampi hitam uditam mahātāpaśūnām paśūnām
śaṁbunambugna pāpa vyatikṛiti bhavatassaprapātāt prapātāt)[58]

In this epigraph, an example of *vinōkti alaṅkāra*, is found in verse sixteen where the poet of this record describes the rule of Māndhāta, one of the kings of the Ikshvāku lineage from whom the Chōḷa kings claimed descent:

'When that king of supreme prowess was ruling this world, the deer wandered in company with the lion, all objects gave up their natural enmity, but righteousness alone did not do so as there was no unrighteousness'.

तस्मिन्नृपे परमतेजसि शासतीनां
भूमिं चकार हरिणा हरिणस्सहापि।
सर्वोमिथस्सहजमप्यजह द्विरोध
धर्मस्वधर्म विरहान्न तथा चकार।।

(*tasmin nṛipē paramatējasi śāsatīnām*
bhūmim chakāra hariṇā hariṇasahāpi,
sarvō mitas sahajam apy ajahād virōdha
dharmastv adharma vīrahāt na tatha chakāra).[59]

One more long lithic inscription of the period of the Chōḷas, belonging to Naralōkavīra, a general of Kulōttuṅga Chōḷa I (1071-1122 A.D.) is found in the Naṭarāja temple at Chidambaram. In this inscription, the various benefactions made by this pious general to this shrine are mentioned in beautiful verses.

One of these verses states that he 'arranged for the offering of the nectar of milk with sugar-candy to the Lord of Gaurī (Śiva), who was given (on a former occasion), poison to drink by the celestials.

क्षीरं सखण्डममृतं कुरुते स्म तस्मिन्
गौरीपतेर्दिविषदो भिषमेवपाया।
भूतप्रज्ञः किममरेषु सभानते किं
भक्तिप्रपञ्च सुलभो भवति प्रसादः।।

(kshīram sakhaṇḍam amritam kurutē sma tasmin
Gourī-patēḥ divishadō bhishamēva pāyā,
bhūta-prajñaḥ kim amarēshu sabhānatē kim,
bhakti prapañcha sulabhō bhavati prasādaḥ).[60]

In another verse in this inscription, the poet states that Naralōkavīra erected a *maṇḍapa* near the sea with huge waves rolling, which looked as though prostrating forwards with folded hands'.

व्यरचयदपि शंभोः मण्डपतीर्थयात्रा
समुचित मुचित यज्ञः स येष पारे समुद्रं।
लुटित लहरि बाहुः यस्य पार्श्वे. पयोधिः
प्रणतिमिव विधत्तेवन्यम प्रक्षयाय।।

(vyarachayadapi Śaṁbōḥ maṇḍapa tīrthayātrā
samuchitamuchita yajñaḥ sa yēsha pārē samudram,
luṭita lahari-bāhuḥ yasya pārśvē payōdhiḥ,
praṇatim iva viddatēvanyama prakshayāya).[61]

One more verse in this epigraph states poetically that Naralōkavīra 'who knew the essence of Śiva worship gave precious jewels which were pure and without any blemish, like the hearts of sages, to adorn the sacred body of the king of Dancers of the Hall (Lord Naṭarāja).

अयमकुरुत तस्मिन् नृत्तराजस्य शंभोः
शिवयजन रसज्ञो मौक्तिकैर्भूषणानि।
वपुषिपरिगतानान् निर्मलानां पुरारेः
मुनिजनहृदयानां यानि साम्यं वहन्ति।।

(ayam akuruta tasmin nṛittarājasya Śaṁbhōḥ,
Śiva–yajana-rasagñō mauktikair bhūshaṇāni,
vapushi parigatānān nirmalānām Purārēh,
munijanahṛidayānām yāni sāmyam vahanti).[62]

Rasas

An example of *bhayānaka rasa* is found in the Karandai inscription where the burning of the city of Mānyakhēṭa (modern Mālkhed, Karnataka) by the army of Rājēndra Chōḷa I is described as follows:

'The divine horde (*dēvas*), abandoning even the celestial abode caught by the ever-consuming flames of the terrible fire burning aloft from that city, probably suddenly fled (away) out of fear, suspecting it to be the fire of the time of the deluge'

त्रिदिवमपि नितान्तम् तत्पुर प्रोत्थितोग्र
ज्वलदनलशिखाभिर्ग्रास्यमानं विहाय।
सुरपरिषदधावत् प्रायशो काण्ड इव
प्रलयसमय वह्निं तर्कयन्ति भयेन।।

(tridivam api nitāntam tat-pura-protthitogra
jvaladana śikhābhir grāsyamānam vihāya,
suraparishad adhāvat prāyaśo kāṇḍa ēva
praḷaya samaya vahnim tarkayanti bhayēna).[63]

Adbhuta-rasa has been well portrayed by the author of the Karandai plates where he mentions the victory of Rājēndra I over the Chālukya king as also his conquest of Kaḍāram (Malaysia) thus:

'It is no wonder that the fire of his prowess burnt (i.e. consumed) the great race of Taila (i.e.) [(1)The Chālukya king of that name; (2) or oil)]; but it is a wonder that having crossed the ocean, it burnt Kaḍāha [(1)The island of Kedah; (2) The vessel of burning called *Kaḍhāi, Kaḍhai* etc.)] which is sealed (*sa-mudra*).

तत् प्रतापदहनोऽदहदुच्चैस्तैलसन्ततिमिति इदं अचित्रम्।
चित्रं अन्यदतिलङ्घ्य समुद्रं दग्धवान् यदुत साधु कडाहम्।।

(*tat – pratāpa – dahano adahad ucchaiḥ taila – santatim iti idam achitram,*

chitram anyad atilanghya samudram daghdavān yaduta sādhu Kaḍāham).[64]

Invocatory Verses

Just like the Pallava and Pāṇḍya copper-plate charters, the Chōḷa epigraphs also begin with a number of verses praising different deities as was the tradition during that period. Stanzas in praise of Brahmā, Vishṇu, Śiva, Pārvatī and Sarasvatī are found in these records.

Vishṇu

In the Chōḷa epigraphs, this deity is referred to by a number of names and epithets like Murāri, Murabhit, Lakshmībharta, Hari, Lakshmīvallabha, Narakāri, Śārṅgin and Kēśava.

Many of the copper-plate grants of the Chōḷa rulers like the Vēḷāñjēri,[65] Anbil,[66] Larger Leiden,[67] Karandai[68] and Kanyākumarī[69] charters commence with invocatory stanzas about Vishṇu.

The Anbil plates open with two verses in praise of this deity. The second and more poetic one in *śārdūlavikrīḍitā* metre is as follows:

'May the arms of Hari, whose extremities glitter over the row of diadems of *dikpālakas* (the guardians of the eight quarters of the universe), while frivolously fondling with them; sportively hanging from which, a multitude of weapons shine throughout the encircling horizon; which expanded (themselves) at the time of the sacrifice performed by Bali; and which resemble in splendour a number of hills of sapphire, give you good fortune as long as the world exists'.

हेलालालितलोकपालमकुठश्रेणीलसत्कोटयो
लोलालंबितहेतिजालविलसद्दिक्चक्रवालान्तराः।
आकल्पं कलयन्तु वो बलिमखव्याजृम्भमाणाहरे
श्रेयांसि त्रिदशेशनीलशिखरि श्रेणीश्रियो बाहवः।।

(hēlā lālita lōkapāla-makuta śrēṇi lasat kōṭayō,
lōlālambita hēti-jāla vilasat dikchakra vālāntarāḥ,
ākalpam kalayantu vo Bali-makha vyājṛimbamāṇa harēś-
śrēyāmsi tridaśēśa nīla śikhari śrēṇī śriyō bāhavaḥ).

In the Kanyākumarī inscription, the third verse in *śragdhara* metre is in praise of Vishṇu and contains *vṛityanuprāsa*, in which some of the letters are repeated and is a delight to read.

'May that Hari, who with his Discus, caused to perish the whole host of the valiant Daityas; who made Bali remain always at the very bottom of the nether regions; who is the protector of the resplendent gods *(suras)*; and who, through you (the king), that are born in this world like a partial incarnation of himself, protects unchallenged in an instant the entire earth-destroy immediately all your sins'.

चक्रे चक्रेण दैत्यप्रकरमतिबलं यस्समस्तं समस्तं
पाता पातालभूलाहित बलिरनिशं भासुराणां सुराणां।

सद्यस्सद्यत्वघं वो हरिरखिलजगद्रक्षणेन क्षणेन
स्वैरं स्वैरं सलेशैरिव धरणिगतै र्संभवद्भिर्भवद्भिः ।।

(chakrē chakrēṇa daitya-prakaramatibalam
yassamastam samastam,
pātā pātāḷabhūlāhita baliraniśam bhāsurāṇām surāṇām,
sadyass sadya tvagam vo Harirakhila jagadrakshaṇena kshaṇena
svyram svyram saleśairiva dharanigatair
ssambhavadbhir bhavadbhiḥ).

Śiva

The Chōḷa epigraphs also contain a large number of verses about Śiva. The imperial Chōḷas starting from the days of Vijayālaya were staunch Śaivities, who built innumerable temples, both big and small, all over the vast Chōḷa empire for their favourite deity and made numerous endowments in the form of gold, jewellery, food-grains and land to these shrines. Therefore, it is not surprising to notice that many of the Chōḷa copper-plate grants, like the Vēḷāñjēri,[70] Anbil,[71] Eśālam[72] and the Kanyākumarī lithic inscription[73] (Chārāla copper-plates) begin with invocatory stanzas praising Śiva.

This deity is referred to in these records by various names, and epithets like Rudra, Śaṁbhu, Ardhēndhumauḷi, Indumauḷi, Śrīkaṇṭha, Śarva, Śaṅkara, Purāntaka, Purāri, Chandraśēkhara, Pinākabhṛit, Dhūrjaṭi, Bhavanīpati, Puradhvit and Sabhāpati.

In the Anbil plates, the poet, Mādhava Bhaṭṭa describes Śiva very beautifully as follows:

'May the club-like arms of him who wears the crescent of the moon (Śiva) which is the function of the dance, cause the alarm of unexpected annihilation of the world in (the minds of) all the gods and demons, terrified at the sound issuing out of the big caverns of the whole circle of hills in the Universe which are drawn (or attracted) with force, and which stretch up to the extreme limits of the circle of the quarters, give you abundant fortune for a long time'.

ये वेगाकृष्ट विश्वाचल वलय महागह्वरोद्यन्निनाद
व्याभीताशेष देवासुरपरिकलिता काण्डसंहार शंकाः।
आशाचक्रावसानावधि परिविसृतास्ताण्डव व्यापृतास्ते
बाह्वदण्डाश्चिरं वो विदधतु महतीं भूतिमर्धेन्दुमौलेः।।

(*yē vegākkṛishṭa viśvāchala valaya mahāgahvarōdyan nināda, vyābhītāsēsha dēvāsura parikalitā kāṇḍa saṁhāra śankhāḥ, āśāchakrāvasāna-avadhi parivisritās tāṇḍava vyāpṛitāst ē bāhadaṇḍāschiram vō vidadhatu mahatīm bhūtim ardhēndu-maulēḥ*).

The poet of the Eśālam inscription begins this record with a beautiful stanza, in *śragdhara* metre about Śiva in his Kalyāṇasundara aspect:

'Let Bhavānīpati, who has obtained in marriage Bhavānī, and who bears appropriate ornaments on his body, the shining eye on his face as *tilaka*, the *kālakūṭa* poison in his throat like a moistened *nīlōtpala* flower, and on the head the digit of the moon as the *chūḍāmaṇi* jewel, give us prosperity'.

श्रीमल्ललाटे तिलकमिववहन् चक्षुरुद्यत् विकासं
कण्ठे सान्द्रेन्द्रनीलोत्पलमिव विदधत् कालकूटं करालं।
मुग्धेन्दुं मूर्ध्नि चूडामणिमिव कलयन् नित्यक्लृप्ताङ्गभूषा
शोभो दिश्यात् भवानीपरिणयनविधिं प्राप्तवान् धूर्जटिर्वः।।

(*Śrīmallalāṭē tilakamiva vahan chakshurudyat vikāsam kaṇtē sāndrēndra nilōtpalamiva vidaddhat kālakūṭam karāḷam, mugdēndum mūrdnim chūḍāmaṇim iva kalayan nitya kliptāṅgabhūshā, śōbhodiśyāt Bhavānī-pariṇayana-vidhim prāptavān Dhūrjaṭir vaḥ*).

Brahmā

Although invocatory verses in praise of Lord Brahmā are by and large, very rarely seen in the inscriptions of the ancient Tamil country, yet a couple of Sanskrit *praśastis* contain stanzas extolling this deity. One such verse is found in the Anbil plates of Parantaka II (Sundara Chōḷa) where the poet Mādhava-Bhaṭṭa describes Brahmā as follows:

'May that light, which is watchful in the sporting act of creating many worlds, which has its sight fixed at the tip of the nose, which has a mass of matted hair with the splendour of lightening, which dwells on the lotus springing out of the navel of the husband of Lakshmī , which is self-crested and which is in the *svastikāsana* posture, fulfill your desire for a long time'

ज्योतिर्जाग्रदनेकलोककरण व्यापारलीलाविधौ
नासाग्रस्फुरदीक्षणं क्षणरुचि श्श्री हारजाटाटवी
लक्ष्मीवल्लभनाभिजात नलिनावासन्तदात्मोद्भवः
ब्रह्म स्वस्तिकमस्तु वश्चिरतरं संकल्प संसिद्धये

(jyōthirjāgrad anēka-lōka-karaṇa-vyāpāra-līlāvidhou,
nāsāgra sphurad īkshaṇam kshaṇaruchish srī-hāra-jāṭāṭavī,
Lakshmī-vallabha nābhi-jāta naḷināvāsantadātmōdbhavaḥ,
Brahmasvstikamastu vaschirataram sankalpa samsiddhayē).[74]

Goddesses

The Chōḷa copper-plate records also contain a few verses about Godesses like Pārvatī and Sarasvatī.

Pārvatī

Among all the Chōḷa inscriptions, there is an invocatory verse about Goddess Pārvatī only in the Tiruvālaṅgāḍu plates. The poet Nārāyaṇa, poetically describes Pārvatī in the *śragdhara* metre utilizing the *śriṅgāra rasa* thus:

'May the bashful Bhavānī (Pārvatī), who seeing her own form (reflected) in the gem on the hood of the king of serpents (which forms) the necklace of Śrīkaṇṭha (Śiva) and (suspecting) it to be another woman, looks askance, excited and jealous of her husband, who, with a heart all-desirous of (her) embrace, prays (for it) bowing at (her) feet, grant you uninterrupted prosperity'.

श्रीकण्ठ कण्ठाभरण भुजगराण्मूर्ध्नि माणिक्य मध्ये
दृष्ट्वात्मीयां सलज्जाप्रतिकृतिमपरांमङ्गनां शङ्कमाना।
आश्लेषालोलचित्तं कृतचरणनति प्रार्थनं वो भवानि
दिश्यात् पश्यन्तधीरन्निजपतिं अनिशं सेर्ष्यमर्धेक्षणेन।।

(Śrīkaṇṭha kaṇṭābharaṇa bhujagarāṇmūrdhni māṇikkya madhyē,
dṛishṭvātmīyām salajjā pratikṛitim aparām aṅganām śaṅkamānā,
āslēśālōlachittam kṛitacharṇanati prārthanam vō Bhavānī
diśyāt paśyantadhiran nija patim aniśam sērshyam ardhēkshaṇēna).[75]

Sarasvatī

Poet Nārayaṇa, begins his two compositions, the Tiruvālaṅgāḍu[76] and Eśālam[77] inscriptions with verses in praise of Sarasvatī, hitherto unseen in the Sanskrit records of the Pallavas and the Paṇḍyas. This composer states in the Tiruvālaṅgaḍu plates in a poetic vein :

'The letters (of the alphabet) limited in number are only fifty; (whereas) the virtues of (the kings of) the solar race are resplendent beyond number. How can I describe these (virtues) with these letters. O! Mother Sarasvatī, secure for me (the help of) other letters (*lipi*) also'

पञ्चाशदेव लिपयः परिवृत्त संख्यान्
संख्यानतीत्य रविवंशगुणाः विभान्ति।
एतैरहं कथममून्कथयामि मह्यं
मातस्सरस्वति लिपीरपरा विधेयाः।।

(pañchāśadēva lipayaḥ parivṛitta saṅkhyān
saṅkhyām atītya, ravi-vaṁśa-guṇāḥ vibhānti
yētair aham katamamūm kathayāmi mahyam,
Māthassarasvati! lipīraparā vidhēyāḥ).

The Eśālam plates echo the very same idea and in almost the same language with only subtle variations.

Echoes from Sanskit Literature

The poets of the Sanskrit inscriptions of the Chōḷa period, just like those who composed similar ones of the Pallava and Pāṇḍya times, display a great deal of familiarity with the epics and Purāṇas as also other Sanskritic texts in their epigraphs.

Once again, as seen in the charters of the previous periods, the poets have drawn extensively from the *Raghuvaṁśa* of Kālidāsa. Since that work deals with the lineage of kings of the Ikshvāku dynasty and the wars fought by them, it possibly appealed to the poets who composed the royal charters of their kings as they too had to eulogize their patrons by writing about their genealogy and their numerous wars. However, apart from the *Raghuvaṁśa,* they also drew inspiration from other works such as Kalīdāsa's *Mēghadūta* and Śaṅkarāchārya's *Saundarya Laharī.*

A verse in the *Raghuvaṁśa* which contains Sunanda's description of the Ikshvāku race:

'In the line of the Ikshvakus, Kakutstha was born, a king among kings, who was eminent for his virtues, from him the high-souled lords of Uttara-Kosala derive their proud title Kakutstha. He derived this title Kakutstha as he sat upon Mahēndra who assumed the form of a bull (*kakud*).'

इक्ष्वाकु वंश्यः ककुदं नृपाणां ककुत्स्थ इत्याहित लक्षणोभूत्
काकुत्स्थशब्दं उन्नतेच्छाः श्लाघ्यं दधन्युत्तर कोशलेन्द्राः
महेन्द्रमास्थाय महोक्षरूपं यः संयति प्राप्तपिनाकिलीलः ।।

(Ikshvāku vaṁśyaḥ kakudam nṛipāṇām
kakustha ityāhita lakshaṇōbūt,
kakutsthaśabdam yatha unnatēcchāḥ
ślāghyam dadattyuttarakōsalēndraḥ
Mahēndram āsthāya mahōksharūpam
yaḥ saṁyati prāpta pinākilīlaḥ).[78]

This has been repeated in a slightly different form in the

Tiruvālaṅgāḍu plates of Rājēndra Chōḷa I whose ancestry is also traced to the Ikshvākus while describing a Chōḷa ancestor called Purañjaya thus:

'As this king, a treasure house of valour, sat on the hump of Indra, who assumed the form of a bull, and thus killed the *asura* soldiers, his name became Kakutstha'.

वृषभरूपधरस्य हरेरसौ ककुदि यत् स्थितवान्निधिरोजसाम्।
युधि जघान सुरेतर सैनिकानजनि तेन ककुत्स्थ समाह्वयः।।

(vṛishabharūpadharasya harērasou kakudhi yatsthitavān-nidhirōjasām,
yudhi jaghāna surētara sainikānajani tēna kakutstha samāhvayaḥ).[79]

The poet Nāṛāyaṇa, composer of the Tiruvālaṅgāḍu plates describes Āditya Chōḷa in a glowing manner and states that 'the earth having sought refuge under the shadow of his matchless white parasol did not experience on any occasion, the pain caused by the heat (of misery).[80]

तस्यैक धवलच्छत्रच्छायामाश्रित्य मेदिनी।
अशर्म धर्म जन्मार्त्तीन्नाभ्यजानात्कदाचन।।

(*tasyaika dhavaḷa chchhatra-chchhāyām aśritya mēdhinī,*
aśarma-dharma-janmārttinnābhyajānāt kadāchana)

and this is very like a verse in the *Raghuvaṁśa* in which one of the successors of Rāma of the Ikshvāku dynasty is described:

'as one whose royal parasol, which had a spotless and serene lusture and which was raised over his head, allayed the fever of the whole world, caused by the loss of the former king'.

तस्यैकस्योच्छ्रितं छत्रं मूर्ध्नि तेनामलत्विषा।
पूर्वराजवियोगौष्म्यं कृत्स्नस्य जगतो हृतम्।।

(*tasyaikasyōchchritam chatram mūrdhni tēnāmalatvisha,*
pūrvarājaviyōgaushmyam kṛitsnasya jagataḥ hṛitam).[81]

Again, a verse in the *Raghuvaṁśa,* which describes the army of king Raghu states:

'By reason of the enjoyment of her waters by the army, which in consequence bore the fragrance of the ichors of elephants, he (Raghu) made the Kāvērī an object of suspicion as it were to the lord of rivers'

स सैन्य परिभोगेण गजदानसुगन्धिना
कावेरीं सरितां पत्युः शङ्कनीयामिवाकरोत्।।

(*sa sainyaparibhōgēṇa gaja-dāna-sugandhinā*
Kāvērīm saritām patyuḥ śaṅkanīyām ivākarōt).[82]

and this finds an echo in the Tiruvālaṅgāḍu plates in which a campaign of Rājēndra Chōḷa is described:

'Rājēndra Chōḷa, with a desire to conquer (enemy kings) reached the Gōdāvarī and by the scented cosmetics on his body (washed away) during a playful bath in the waters (of that river) caused her (i.e. the Gōdāvarī) to be suspected (of enjoyment with a stranger), by the lord of rivers (i.e. the ocean)'

गोदावरीमभ्यसरत् स्त्रवन्तीं राजेन्द्रचोलोविजिगीषयासौ
स्वांगांगरागैर्ज्जलकेलिकायां सरित्पतेस्तामकरोच्च शंकाम्।।

(*Gōdāvarīmabhyasaratsravantīm Rājēndra Chōḷō vijigīsha yāsou, svāngānga-rāgairjala-kēḷikāyām saritpatēsstām akarōccha śankām*).[83]

Nārāyaṇa, the poet of the Larger Leiden plates describes Parāntaka I, the son of Āditya Chōḷa I thus:

'From him (i.e. Āditya), who was the sole abode of countless heap of gems (and) who possessed enormous strength, rose for the benefit of the world, king Parāntaka, with full glory, just as the moon does, with all his rays, to give pleasure to the world, from the milky ocean which contains within it countless gems and huge aquatic animals.'

अनन्त रत्न प्रकरैकवासादुदारसत्वादुदियाय तस्मात्।
परान्तको विश्वहिताय राजा राजेव दुग्धाम्बुनिधे कलाभिः।।
*(ananta-ratna-prakaraikavāsād udārasatvād udiyāya tasmāt,
Parāntakō viśvahitāya rājā rājēva dugdhāmbunidhēḥ kalābhiḥ)*.[84]

and this is similar to the second half of a verse in the *Raghuvaṁśa* in which king Dilīpa is described as inspiring awe and confidence just as the ocean which has in it countless gems and large aquatic animals.

अघृष्याश्चाभिगम्यश्च यादोरत्नैरिवार्णवः
(agrishyaśchābhigamyascha yādō ratnairivārṇavaḥ).[85]

Apart from the *Raghuvaṁśa*, the poets of these inscriptions appear to have drawn from other sources also. In the Tiruvālaṅgāḍu plates, the poet while describing the city of Tañjāvūr, mentions poetically that this city had reached the sky (by its high turrets).

व्याप्तांबराम्
vyāptāmbarām [86]

and it is possible that this may be an echo of a verse in the *Mēghadūta*, where poet Kālidāsa describes the city of Alaka (Alakāpuri) as having 'domes which touch the sky'.

तुङ्गमभ्रंलिहाग्राः
(tuṅgam abhram lihāgrāhāḥ).[87]

The inscription of Naralōkavīra at Chidambaram mentioned earlier in this chapter, also contains echoes of Kālidāsa's works.

A verse in this inscription states that Naralōkavīra 'built two tall towers reaching out to the sky from which flags flew majestically as if inviting people from different quarters to take shelter there from the scorching heat of the sun.'

अस्यायं स चकार गोपुरयुगं या मेघ तुङ्गं स्थिरं
प्राकारस्य यदग्रकेतनपठाः प्रेङ्खेलिता वायुभिः।

भानो सानुना वैद्यमेतदुदितं तामुञ्चशंकां क्रमात्
आगच्छेति दिशां मुखेष्वभिनयं संवर्तयन्तीव ते।।

(asyāyam sa chakāra gōpurayugam yā mēgha-tuṅgam sthiram,
prākārasya yadagra kētana paṭāḥ prēṅkēḷitā vāyubhiḥ,
bhānō sānuna vaidyamētad uditam tā muñcha śaṅkām kramāt,
āgachchēti diśām mukēshvabhinayam saṁvartayantīva tē).[88]

This verse is a fine example of *utprēksha alaṅkāra* and also echoes of ideas found in Kālidāsa's *'Abijñāna Śākuntalam'* where the heroine Śakūntalā mentions that 'a kesāra tree appears to be hurrying me to it with the fingers of its leaves, set in motion by the wind'.

वातेरितपल्लवाङ्गुलीभिः त्वरयतीव मां केसरवृक्षः।।

(vātērita pallavāngulībhiḥ tvarayatīva mām kēsara vṛikshaḥ).[89]

In this same inscription of Naralōkavīra, there is a line in verse 18, mentioned earlier which states that he 'gave pearls to Lord Naṭarāja which were like the hearts of the sages, pure and without blemish'

अयमकुरुत तस्मिन् नृत्तराजस्य शंभोः
शिवयजन रसज्ञो मौक्तिकैर्भूषणानि।
वपुषिपरिगतानान् निर्मलानां पुरारेः
मुनिजन हृदयानां यानि साम्यं वहन्ति।।

(ayam akuruta tasmin nṛittarājasya Śambhōḥ,
Śiva–yajana-rasagñō mauktikaiḥ bhūshaṇāni,
vapushi parigatānān nirmalānām Purārēh,
munijana-hṛidayānām yāni sāmyam vahanti).[90]

appears to be an echo of a verse in the *Vālmīki Rāmāyaṇam*, in which the poet describing the Tamasa river states: 'the clear water of Tamasa was like the hearts of noble men which is pure.'

रमणीयं प्रसन्नाम्बु सन्मनुष्य मनोयथा।।

(ramaṇīyam prasanāṁbu sanmanushyamanō yatha).[91]

Metres used in the Chōḷa Inscriptions

1 *Vēḷāñjeri plates of Parāntaka Chōla I* (c. 932 A.D)
v.1, 8 Śārdūlavikriḍita; vv.2,14-Śragdhara; vv.3, 9 – Mandākrānta; v.4 – Upēndravajra; v.6-Svāgatā; vv.7, 12, 13 – Vasantatilakā; vv.10, 11, 15, 16 – Anushṭubh

2 *Anbil plates of Parāntaka II (Sundara Chōḷa)* (961 A.D)
v-1- Mandākrāntā; vv.2, 4, 5, 12, 20, 24, 25, 28, - Śārdūlavikrīḍita; vv.3, 13, 18, 27, 30, 32, 33, 44, 46 - Śragdhara; v.6, 31, - Vasantatilakā; v.7 – Pushpitāgrā; v.8- Hariṇī; vv.9, 14-16, 26, 34, 36, 38-41 – Anushṭubh; v.10 Rathōddhatā; v.11- Mañjubhāshiṇī; vv.17 & 35 – Praharshiṇī; v.19 – Upēndravajra; vv.21, 23, 43 - Āryā; v.22 – Sundarī; v.29 – Vaṁśastha; v.37 – Upajāti; v.42 Indravajra; v.45-Svāgatā

3 *Larger Leiden plates of Rājarāja Chōḷa I* (1006 A.D)
vv.7, 8, 11, 14, 23, 26, 27, 35-37, 40-45, 47 & 48 – Anushṭubh; v.32-Mālabhāriṇi; vv.12, 21, 30 & 39 – Mandākrāntā; v.13 – Mañjubhāshiṇi; v.9 – Praharshiṇī; v.10 – Rathōddhatā; v.24-Ruchira; vv.1, 4, 18, 19 & 33 - Śārdūlavikrīḍitā; vv.2, 3, 20–Sragdharā; vv. 5,6,15,17,22,28,34,38 &46-Upajāti; v.29-Vaṁsasthā; vv.16,25 &31-Vasantatilakā.

4 *Tiruvālaṅgāḍu plates of Rājēndra Chōḷa I* (1018 A.D)
vv.1, 2, 71, 137 - Śragdhara; vv-3, 7, 13, 38, 51, 87, 97, 101, 103, 104, 125 – Vasantatilakā; vv. 4, 12, 19, 25, 45, 47, 50, 55, 77, 81, 82, 93, 99, 100, 102, 118, 119, 126 – Indravajra; vv.5, 9, - Praharshiṇī; vv.6, 15, 61, 69, 72, 117 – Mālinī; vv.8, 62 – Drutavilambita; vv. 10, 18, 23, 26, 29, 37, 52, 63, 64, 88, 108, - Svāgata; v.11- Āryā; vv.14, 35, 36 – Kāmamatha; vv.16, 43, 80 Mandākrānta; vv.17, 27, 28, 42, 65, 83, 84, 127 - Śārdūlavikrīḍita; vv.20, 30-34, 40, 48, 58, 60, 66, 68, 75, 99, 121, 124, 128, 129, 130, 134, 136, - Anushṭubh; vv.21, 74, 113, 120, 122, 123 – Viyōginī; vv.39, 44, 53, 59, 70, 76, 85, 89-92, 94-96, 105, 106, 111, 112, 114-116- Pushpitāgra; v.46 – Vaṁśastha; v.54-Śalinī; v.59-

Hariṇī; vv.57, 98, 110 – Upēndravajra; vv.78, 79, 135 - Ārya; v.109-Indrōpēndra; v.117 – Mañjubhāshiṇi.

5 *Karandai plates of Rājēndra Chōḷa I* (1021 A.D.) vv.1,2,27,29,34-36,46,58,68,70-Śārdūlavikrīḍita; vv.3,47,53,55-57,75-Śragdhara; vv.4,9,11,13,15,20-22,28,30-32,40,50,52,60,69,76-Anushṭubh; vv.5,14,17,24,25,49,64,71,73-Vasantatilakā; vv. 6, 7, 16, 18, 19, 33, 37, 38, 41, 44, 48, 51 and65-Upajāti; v.8-Viyōgini; vv.10,54-Mālini; vv.12 &43-Pushpitāgra; v.23-Ruchira; vv.26, 66, 67, 72-Mandākrāntā; v.39-Pramatitākshara; v.42-Vaṁsasthavilā; vv.45&61-Manjubhāshiṇī; v.59-Pṛithvi; v. 62-Svāgata;v.63-Rathoddhata;v. 74-Praharshiṇī.

6. *Eśālam plates of Rājēndra Chōḷa I* vv.1, 3, 13 - Sragdhara; vv.2, 10, 24, 26, 32, 33 - Vasantatilakā; vv.4, 6, 14, 17, 20, 23, 25, 31 – Śārdūlavikrīḍitā; vv.5, 12 – Mālini; vv.7, 21, 34 – Anushṭubh; v.8 – Pushpitāgra; v.11 – Upēndravajra; vv.15, 28, Upajāti; v.16 Mandākrāntā; vv.18, 35 – Āryā; v.29 – Svāgatā.

7 *Kanyākumarī Inscription of Vīra-Rājēndra Chōḷa* (1069 A.D) vv.1, 10-12, 18, 21, 24, 26, 44, 47, 52, 56, 73, 76, 77, 79 - Śārdūlavikrīḍitā; vv.2-9, 15, 20, 60 - Śragdhara; v.13-Vaṁśastha; vv.14, 49, 71 - Śikhariṇi; vv.16, 48, 50, 57, 67, 72, 74 – Vasantatilakā; vv.17, 23, 25, 41, 62, 65, 69 – Mālinī; vv.19, 27, 28, 40, 75 – Mandākrāntā; vv.22, 53, 78 - Śvāgatā; vv.30, 31, 61 – Pṛithvi; vv.32, 46, 59 – Praharshiṇī; vv.33, 38, 39, 42 - Śālini; vv. 34-35 – Hariṇī; vv.36-37, 58, 63, 66, 68 – Rathōddhata; vv.43, 54, 55 – Upajāti ; vv.51, 64, 70 – Upēndravajra; vv. 80 and 81 – Anushṭubh; vv.29, 45-Aupachchhandaśika.

Chidambaram, Inscription of Naralokavīra

v.1, 8-10, 23, 26, 27 - Śārdūlavikrīḍita; vv.2, 4-6, 13,16-18 – Mālinī; vv.3, 31 – Mandākrāntā; vv.7, 12-22, 24 – Vasantatilaka; vv.11, 29, 30 – Indravajra; v.14 – Pṛithvi; v.25 – Anushṭubh; v. 28 - Śragdhara.

REFERENCES

1. R. Nagaswamy, *Tiruttani and Vēḷāñjēri plates*, Madras, 1979.
2. *E.I*, Vol. XV, No. 5, pp. 58-64 (Anbil Plates of Sundara Chōḷa).
3. *E.I.*, Vol. XXII, No. 34, pp. 238-243 (Larger Leiden plates of Rājarāja I).
4. *S.I.I.*, Vol. III, No. 205, pp. 393-401 (Tiruvālaṅgāḍu copper plates of Rājēndra Chōḷa I).
5. K.G. Krishnan '*Karandai Tamil Sangam Plates of.Rājēndra Chōḷa I*', New Delhi, 1984.
6. R. Nagaswamy, '*Bulletin De 'Ecole Francaise*' (D'Extreme – Orient), Tome LXXVI, Paris, (Eśālam Copper-plates of Rājēndra I).
7. *E.I.*, Vol. XVIII, No. 4, pp. 31-47 (Kanyākumarī Inscription of Vīra-Rājēndradēva).
8. *E.I.*, Vol. XXV, No. 25, pp. 254-362 (Chārāla plates of Vīra-Rājēndradēva).
9. *S.I.T.I.* Vol. III, Part II, pp. 1304-24.
10. *A.R.E.*, 473 of 1919.
11. *S.I.I.*, Vol. XXVI, No. 388, p. 253.
12. Karandai plates, *op. cit.*, v. 42, p. 72.
13. *S.I.I.*, Vol. II, Nos. 12 & 13, pp. 97-99.
14. T.V. Sadasiva Pandarathar, '*History of the Later Chōḷas*, Annamalainagar, 1949.
15. R. Nagaswamy, *Tiruttani and Vēḷāñjēri plates*, Plate V, p. 2.
16. *E.I.*, Vol. IV, No. 32, v.10, p. 224 (Shōḷingūr Rock Inscription of Parāntaka I).
17. Anbil plates, *op.cit.*, v. 46, p. 64.
18. Larger Leiden plates, *op.cit.*, p. 228.
19. *Ibid.*, v. 39, p. 242.
20. Tiruvālaṅgāḍu plates, *op.cit.*, v. 136, p. 401.
21. Karandai plates, *op.cit.*, v. 76, p. 76.
22. Eśālam plates, *op.cit.*, v. 34, p. 33.
23. K.G. Krishnan, *op.cit.*, p. 53.
24. Eśālam plates, *op.cit.*, p. 26.
25. *Ibid.*, p. 27.

26. Kanyākumarī inscription, *op.cit.*, pp. 129-149.
27. Chārāla plates, *op.cit.*, v. 83, p. 264.
28. *Ibid.*, v. 87.
29. *S.I.T.I.*, Vol. III, pt. II, pp.1304 – 24.
30. *S.I.I.* Vol. XXVI, No. 388, p. 253.
31. R. Nagaswamy, *TVCP*, Plate II, v.12.
32. *Ibid.*, v.13.
33. Anbil plates, *op.cit.*, v. 27, pp. 61–62.
34. *Ibid.*, v. 30.
35. *Ibid.*, v. 20.
36. Larger Leiden plates, *op-cit.*, v. 21, p. 240.
37. *Ibid.*, v. 22.
38. *Ibid.*, v. 27.
39. Tiruvālaṅgāḍu plates, *op.cit.*, v. 23, p. 394.
40. *Ibid.*, v.10.
41. *Ibid.*, v.18.
42. *Ibid.*, v. 52, p. 396.
43. *Ibid.*, v. 63 (By this, the poet refers to the mythological story of Ādiśēsha, the king of serpents, who is believed to uphold the weight of the earth. The Nāgā women are mentioned here as his wives.)
44. *Ibid.*, v. 64, p. 397 .
45. *Ibid.*, v. 65.
46. *Ibid.*, v. 68.
47. *Ibid.*, v. 75.
48. *Ibid.*, v. 81, p. 398 (The learned editor of this inscription has commented that *taila* means oil, and it is natural for a liquid to flow or run).
49. *Ibid.*, v. 101, p. 399.
50. *Ibid.*, v. 102.
51. *Ibid.*, v. 103.
52. *Ibid.*, v.115, p. 400.
53. Karandai plates, *op.cit.*, v. 34, p. 72.
54. *Ibid.*, v. 38 (According to Hindu mythology, the four quarters (i.e.), east, south, west and north are guarded by Indra, Yama, Varuṇa and Kubēra respectively).

55. *Ibid.*, v. 41.
56. *Ibid.*, v. 72, p. 75.
57. Eśālam plates, *op.cit.*, v.16, p. 32.
58. Kanyākumarī inscription, *op.cit.*, v. 2, p. 32.
59. *Ibid.*, v.16, p. 35.
60. *S.I.T.I.*, Vol. II, Part III, v.19, p.1315.
61. *Ibid.*, v. 6, p. 1306.
62. *Ibid.*, v. 18, p. 1315.
63. Karandai plates, *op.cit.*, v. 54, p. 73.
64. *Ibid.*, v. 62, p. 74.
65. R. Nagaswamy, *TVCP*, v. 1, Plate I.
66. Anbil plates, *op.cit.*, vv.1-2, p. 58.
67. Larger Leiden plates, *op.cit.*, v. 1, p. 238.
68. Karandai plates, *op.cit*, v. 1, p. 69
69. Kanyākumarī inscription, *op.cit.*, v. 3, pp. 129-30.
70. R. Nagaswamy, *op.cit.*, v. 2, Plate I.
71. Anbil plates, *op.cit.*, v.3, p. 59.
72. Eśālam plates, *op.cit.*, v.1, p. 31.
73. Kanyākumarī inscription, *op.cit.*, vv.1-2, pp. 31-32.
74. Anbil plates, *op.cit*, v.4, p. 59.
75. Tiruvālaṅgāḍu plates, *op.cit*, v. 1, p. 393.
76. *Ibid.*, v. 3
77. Eśālam plates *op.cit.*, v. 2, p. 31.
78. Venkataraghavachariar, V. (Ed.) *Raghuvamśa Mahākāvya*, Madras, 1991, Sarga VI.72.
79. Tiruvālaṅgāḍu plates, *op.cit.*, v.8, p.393; C. Sivaramamurti, *Epigraphical Echoes of Kalidāsa*, Madras, 1944, pp. 31-32
80. Tiruvālaṅgāḍu plates, *op.cit.*, v. 48, p. 396.
81. *Raghuvaṁśa*, *op.cit.*, Sarga XVII. 33.
82. *Ibid.*, Sarga IV.45.
83. Tiruvālaṅgāḍu plates, *op.cit.*, v. 118, p. 400.
84. Larger Leiden plates, *op.cit.*, v. 15, p. 239.
85. *Raghuvaṁśa*, *op.cit.*, Sarga I.16.
86. Tiruvālaṅgāḍu plates, *op.cit.*, v. 45, p. 395.
87. Kale, M.R., *Mēghadūta* (Text and Translation), Delhi, 1991, Uttaramēgha, v.1, p. 109.

88. *S.I.T.I.*, Vol. II, Part. III, v. 59, p. 1309.
89. Kale, M.R. (Translation), *Abijñāna Śākuntalam* of *Kāḷidāsa*, Delhi, 2000, Act. I, p. 26.
90. *S.I.T.I.*, Vol. II, Part III, v. 18, p. 1315.
91. Gargil, Amarendra Lakshmana (Ed.), *Śrīmad Vālmīki Rāmāyaṇam*, Pune, 1982, *Bālakāṇḍa*, Sarga II, v.5

4

Other Inscriptions

Apart from the Sanskrit *praśastis* and the epigraphs which are wholly in Sanskrit of the Pallava, Chōḷa and Pāṇḍya periods, there are some Sanskrit epigraphs belonging to the vassal-chiefs who were subordinate to these imperial powers, found inscribed on the walls of temples as well as on copper-plate charters. There are also a few Sanskrit epigraphs of kings from outside the Tamil country who ruled over some parts of ancient Tamil Nadu for short periods.

Among the vassal chieftains of the ancient Tamil country, one of the earliest Sanskrit records is that of Bhk̄uti Vikrama Kēsari,[1] a subordinate of Āditya Chōla I (c. 871-907 A.D.) and his son and successor, Parāntaka Chōla I[2] (907-955 A.D.) engraved in the temple of Mūvarkōvil, in Koḍuṁbālūr (Pudukkoṭṭai) which he constructed.

Another interesting epigraph is the Udayēndiram copper-plate inscription of Pṛithivipati II Hastimalla,[3] who was a vassal of Parāntaka Chōḷa I. This bi-lingual record, which has twenty-eight verses in the Sanskrit *praśasti* section gives the genealogy of this Western Gaṅga chieftain on whom the Bāṇa kingdom had been confered by his king Parāntaka I. Another copper-plate record which is fully in

Sanskrit belongs to the Bāṇa chieftain, Vikramāditya II[4] of the period of Kulōttuṅga Chōḷa III (1178-1217 A.D.). There are a number of Sanskrit epigraphs of a Bāṇa chieftain named Rājarājadēvan which have been engraved in several temples like Tiruvānnaikāval, Tiruvaṇṇāmalai and at other places in North and South Arcot districts.

There are also many stone epigraphs of the Hoysala rulers of Karnataka who conquered some parts of the ancient Tamil country found at places like Śrīraṅgam and Kāñchīpuram.

There are also records of the Kēraḷa ruler Ravivarman Kulaśēkhara (1299-1314 A.D.), and of a Saṁbhuvarāya chieftain called Vīra-Chaṁpa of the 14th century A.D. found at different places in Tamil Nadu.

In this chapter, the focus will be on the analysis of the above-mentioned inscriptions.

Poets

One of the earliest Sanskrit epigraphs of the vassals of the Chōḷas is the Mūvarkōvil record of Bhūti Vikrama Kēsari, but unfortunately this inscription, as well as the Udayēndiram copper-plate grant of Pṛithivipati II Hastimalla, the Western Gaṅga vassal of Parāntaka I and the Udayēndiram plates of the Bāṇa chieftain Vikramāditya II do not contain the names of the talented poets who wrote these records.

It is only when we come to the period of Kulōttuṅga Chōḷa III that we come across the name of a poet who composed some of the Sanskrit inscriptions of his vassal named Rājarājadēvan alias Magadaināḍāḷvān and Poṇpaparappināṉ (on account of his having covered the shrine of Lord Aruṇāchalēśvara at Tiruvaṇṇāmalai with gold).

Several inscriptions of this chieftain have been discovered at the Jambukēśvara temple at Tiruvānaikkāval

(Tiruchirāpaḷḷi district),[5] Aruṇachalēśvara temple at Tiruvaṇṇāmalai (South Arcot district),[6] Kailāsanātha temple at Nārattampūṇḍi (North Arcot district),[7] at Aragaṇḍanallūr,[8] and the Subrahmaṇya temple at Tirupparaṅkuṇḍram (Madurai district).[9] They were composed by a poet who held the title Vidyāchakravartin and from his records we find his titles such as Kavirāja, Sakalavidyāchakravartin, Sakalavidyādharachakravartin and Tribhuvanakavichakravartin.

S.S. Janaki has identified this poet with a person named Karpagavilli mentioned in two records from the Puṇḍarīkāksha Perumāḷ temple in Tiruveḷḷarai (Tiruchirapalli district) dated 1209 and 1213 A.D. belonging to the period of Kulōttuṅga Chōḷa III.[10] These inscriptions speak of a Karpagavilli maṭha, named after the donor and that this person arranged for feeding nine-hundred people in this maṭha during certain festival days. This poet was obviously financially secure as seen from his inscription found at Nāratāmpūṇḍi which mentions that he was rewarded with lordly elephants for his compositions.

बाणेश्वरं प्रति कविराजराजेन सकलविद्या-चक्रवर्तिना, विरचितानि मत्तकुञ्जरमूल्यानि पद्यानि

(*Bāṇēśvaram prati kavirāja-rājēna sakalavidyāchakravartinā virachitāni mattakuñjara-mūlyāni padyāni*).[11]

The Tiruvaḷḷarai records also mention that he was the performer of the Vājapēya sacrifice (*Vājapēyayājin*). He was probably the author of the commentary *Dīpa* on the *Drahyāyaṇa Śrauta Sūtra.*[12]

Apart from this poet, many of the other members of his family, who were also talented composers, held the title Vidyāchakravartin. One of these was the author of the Sanskrit historical prose work *Gadyakarṇāmṛita* and has been considered to be the same person as Sokkavilli mentioned in some inscriptions from the Raṅganāthasvāmi temple,

Śrīraṅgam of the period of the Hoysala ruler, Vīra-Rāmanātha (1254-1295 A.D.).[13] These inscriptions refer to Sokkavilli Bhaṭṭa by the title Sakalavidyāchakravartin and mention an expensive gift given by him to Lord Raṅganātha.

One more Vidyāchakravartin, the composer of the *Rukmiṇīkalyāṇa*, commentaries on the *Kāvyaprakāśa*, *Alaṅkāraśarvasva*, the *Prayōgadīpikā* and other literary works was the contemporary of the Hoysala king Ballāla III (1291-1342 A.D.), who also composed an inscription in Sanskrit of the period of this ruler, found at Kāñchīpuram.[14]

A number of Sanskrit inscriptions of the Kēraḷa ruler, Ravivarman Kulaśēkhara who ruled briefly over some parts of the Tamil country have been discovered at several shrines like the Raṅganāthasvāmi temple in Śrīraṅgam,[15] the Varadarājasvāmi temple at Kāñchīpuram[16] and at Tiruvaḍi (South Arcot district).[17] They were composed by a poet named Kavibhūshaṇa.

An inscription of a chieftain named Vīra-Chaṁpa, found at the Varadarājasvāmi temple, Kāñchīpuram[18] mentions that it was composed by this chieftain's minister, Vanabhid. Another epigraph of this same chieftain engraved in the Bilvanāthasvāmi temple at Tiruvallam (North Arcot district), which unfortunately does not mention the composer appears to have been composed by the same poet, since the language closely resembles that of the Varadarājasvāmi temple record.[19]

Literary Beauty

Although the records of the vassal chiefs and other kings, apart from the Pallava, Pāṇḍya and Chōḷa rulers found in Tamil Nadu, do contain some verses of literary merit, yet we find that they do not reach the level of excellence exhibited by the poets employed by the imperial houses to compose their records. Just like in the other epigraphs, most of the verses are in praise of the kings, and in some of them, the poets have shown their skill with words. As mentioned earlier, probably the earliest Sanskrit record of the vassals of the Chōḷas is the Koḍuṁbāḷūr inscription of Bhūti Vikrama Kēsari. This record is composed in excellent Sanskrit and gives the genealogy of Vikrama Kēsari and his achievements. In one stanza, the poet very beautifully describes his king and the state of his kingdom when he ruled:

'While the earth was ruled by him, the Kalpataru (wishing tree) to the learned, the moon to the lilies, viz. the two hands of the subordinate kings and the beloved of the Goddess of the Earth, victory, prosperity, fame and speech; sharpness was found (only) in the pair of eyes, instability in the two eyelashes and darkness in the hair (of women) and weakness in their bodies'.

विद्वत् कल्पतरौ क्षितीश्वर कर द्वन्द्वाम्भुजेन्दो भुवं
यस्मिन् शाशति मेदिनी जयरमा श्रीकीर्ति वाग्वल्लभे।
तैक्ष्ण्यं नेत्रयुगे भ्रुवोश्चलनता केशेषु कार्ष्यान्तनौ
तन्वीनां तनुताभवत् स्तनयुगे च अन्योन्य संपीडनम्।।

(vidvat-kalpatarau kshitīśvarakara-dvandvāmbhujēndau bhuvam
yasmin śāsati mēdhinī jaya-ramā-śrī-kīrti-vāg-vallabhē,
taikshṇyam nētrayugē bruvōschalanatā kēśēshu kārshṇyāntanao
tanvīnām tanutābhavat sthanayugē cha anyōnya sampīḍanam).[20]

In th. Udayēndiram plates of Pṛithivipati II, there is a beautiful verse praising this ruler:

'Oppressed by the Kali (age), the crowd of virtues, *viz.*, courage, liberality, gratitude, sweetness, courtesy, wisdom, patience, intelligence, purity, tranquility, dignity, mercy, forbearance, etc., forthwith joined, in order to rest without grief and fatigue, in this Pṛithivipati, because they thought that he was born of the race of Bali'.

शौर्य्योदार्य कृतज्ञता मधुरता दाक्षिण्य मेधाक्षमा
प्रज्ञाशौच शमानुभाव करुणा क्षान्ति प्रधानो नयी
आक्रान्त पृथिवीपतिं स कलिना शोकावसादौ विना
स्थातुं प्राग्बलिवंशजोयमिति यम् भेजे गुणानां गणः।।

(*śouryōdārya kṛitagñatā madhuratā dākshiṇya mēdhā kshamā prajñāśaucha śamānubhāva karuṇā kshānti pradhānō nayī, ākrānta Pṛithivīpatim sa kalinā śōkāvasādou vinā, sthātum prāgbalivamśajōyam iti yam bhējē guṇānām gaṇaḥ*).[21]

The next verse of this inscription, also very poetic, contains *slēśa*:

'He deservedly bore the other name Hastimalla as he tore up the hill-chiefs, together with the Pallavas, as he was devoted to virtus, as his fingers (always) carried gifts, as he bore the earth (and) as he was prosperous from birth: (just as the divine elephant Airāvata tears up large hills like sprouts, is beloved by Indra, carries rut on the tip of his trunk, bears the earth, and was born (from the milk ocean) together with the Goddess of Prosperity'.

विदारयन् पल्लववद्गिरीन्द्रान् वृषप्रियो दानवह्यग्रहस्तः।
वहन्महीं श्रीसहजो यथार्थं यो हस्तिमल्लापर नामधेयः।।

(*vidārayan Pallavavadgirīndrān vṛishapṛiyō dhānavahāgra-hastaḥ, vahanmahīm śrīsahajō yathārtham yō Hastimallāpara nāmadheyaḥ*).[22]

In one of the inscriptions of the poet Sakalavidyā-chakravartin who composed the verses for his patron, the Bāṇa chief, Rājarājadēvan alias Magadaipperumāḷ, engraved on a *gōpura* in the Aruṇāchalēśvara temple in Tiruvaṇṇāmalai, this composer states very poetically that this Bāṇa chieftain took away the crown of the Pāṇḍyas six times, and that he handed over only one of them to the Chōḷa king (who was his overlord). The poet adds that the munificent Bāṇa chief offered the other five crowns to Aruṇāchala, (the presiding deity of Tiruvaṇṇāmalai), and being thus dispossessed, had nothing to offer to his supplicants.

पूर्वं पञ्चकमद्य चैकममरक्ष्मापालगर्वद्रुहः
पाण्ड्यात् संयति संहृतानि मकुटान्येतेषु बाणेश्वर।
एकञ्चोलकृते वितीर्णमपराण्यद्यारुणाख्यायते
शैलेन्द्राय समर्पितानि भवता किं वार्तिने दास्यते।।

(pūrvam pañchakamadya chaikamamara-kshmāpāla-garva druhaḥ,
Pāṇḍyātsaṁyati saṁhṛitāni makuṭānyētēshu Bāṇēśvara,
yēkañchōḷakṛitē vitīrṇamaparāṇadyāruṇākhyātē,
Śailēndrāya samarpitāni bhavatā kiṁ vārthinē dāsyatē).[23]

In another verse at the same place, this composer, while describing his king's devotion to Lord Śiva at Tiruvaṇṇāmalai, states that this Bāṇa chieftain, having won over all the kings and collected bounties from them, covered Aruṇādri with gold, and thus, the sun mistook it for the Mēru mountain and circumambulated it.

जित्वा बाहुवलेन बाहुजवलान्याच्छिद्यनीवीधनं
तेन स्वर्णमयेश्वराय रचिते बाणारूणाद्रौत्वया।
संभ्रान्त्या भुवनस्य किं त्रिभुवन भ्रान्तिप्रतिक्षेपकः
पूषा भ्राम्यति मेरुभूधरधिया सव्यप्रयाणोद्यतः।।

(jitvā bāhubalēna bāhujabalānāchidya nīvīdhanam
tēna svarṇamayēśvarāya rachitē Baṇāruṇādrou tvayā,
saṁbhrāntyā bhuvanasya kim tribhuvana bhrānti-pratikshēpakaḥ
pūshā bhrāmyati mēru-bhūdharadiyā savya prayaṇōdhyataḥ).[24]

Invocatory Verses

Among the epigraphs analyzed in this chapter, very few records begin with invocatory verses, as they are mostly lithic inscriptions. However, the Udayēndiram copper-plates of Pṛithivipati II and the copper-plates of Bāṇa Vikramāditya II contain beautiful stanzas in praise of Vishṇu and Śiva.

Vishṇu

The first verse of Pṛithivipati's record embodies the concept of Harihara (or Śaṅkaranārāyaṇa), the combined form of Vishṇu and Śiva and runs as follows:

'May He (Vishṇu), incessantly grant you prosperity, the lord of prosperity (and) master of the Universe, of whom the eight-bodied (Śiva) himself became one half of the body; from the lotus on whose navel the creator of the worlds was produced; (and) whose true nature, the primeval speech (i.e., the Vēda) reveals.'

यस्याष्टमूर्तिरभवत् स्वयमर्द्धमूर्तिः
यन्नाभिपंकजभुवो जगतां प्रसूतिः।
यस्यानिशं प्रथमवाग्विवृणोति तत्त्वं
स श्रीधरो दिशतु विश्वपतिः श्रियं वः।।

(yasyāshṭa-mūrtirabhavat svayamardha-mūrtir-
yannābhi-pañkaja-bhavō-jagatām prasūtiḥ,
yasyāniśam pratamavāgvivṛiṇōti tatvam
sa Śrīdharō diśatu viśva-patiḥ śriyamvaḥ).[25]

A verse in Bāṇa Vikramāditya's inscription also gives a glorious description of Vishṇu;

'May that Nārāyaṇa, whose body ever rests on the lord of serpents, (and) whose two feet are worshipped by crowds of Gods, guard you. He, whom the Gods and the demons, desirous of churning the matchless sea of milk, discarding the Mandara laid hold of, as it were, to obtain, a second time the nectar of immortality, (and) who then shone, even more than ordinary, as if he were, the Añjana mountain'.

क्षीरोदं मथितुं मनोभिरतुलं देवास्सुरैर्मन्दरं
हित्वा क्षिप्त इव अञ्जनाद्रिरिव यस्तत्राधिकं राजते।
यो भोगीन्द्रनिविष्ट मूर्तिरनिशं भूयोऽमृतास्याप्तये
रक्षेद्वः सुरवृन्द वन्दित पद द्वन्द्वस्स नारायणः।।

(kshīrōdam mathitum manōbhiratulam dēvāsurairmandaram,
hitvākshipta iva Añjanādririva yaḥ tatrādhikam rājatē,

yō bhōgīndra nivishṭa mūrtiraniśam bhūyō-amṛitāsyāptayē rakshēt vaḥ surabrinda-vandita-pada-dvandvaḥ saḥ Nārāyaṇaḥ).[26]

Śiva

There are also some beautiful stanzas about Śiva in some of the copper-plate grants of the vassal chiefs. In the inscription of Prithivīpati II there is a verse in praise of Śiva as follows:

'Let Him remove your sins, the being (Śiva), who is the enemy of Cupid, whose diadem is the moon, the dark spot on whose throat resembles a particle of a cloud; (and) in whose forehead is sunk a (third) reddish eye'.

मारवैरिमधुरांशु शेखरन्नीरवाहलवनील कन्धरम्।
भालमग्न कपिलेक्षणं वपुर्द्दूरतो हरतु दुष्कृतानि वः।।

(*māra-vairi madhurāmśu-śēkharannīravāhalava-nīlakandharam,*
bhāla-magna kapilēkshaṇam vapurddūratō
haratu dushkṛitāni vaḥ).[27]

Similarly, there is another verse in the copper-plate grant of the Bāṇa chieftain Vikramāditya II about Śiva:

'May that Śiva promote your well-being, whose true nature even the Vēda cannot fully reveal, from whom the creation, preservation and the destruction of all the worlds proceed, on whom the devotees meditate (and) whose two feet are tinged with the collections of red rays of the rows of jewels in the diadems of the crowds of the chiefs of the Gods who in person bow down before him!'

यत्तत्व प्रकटीकृतौ अतितरां वेदोपि नालं यतः
स्थित्युत्पत्ति लयस्समस्त जगतां यन्मन्वते योगिनः।
साक्षान्नम्र सुरेन्द्र वृन्दमकुट व्यालीन रत्नावली
शोणांशु व्रजरञ्जितांघ्रि युगलो भूत्यै शिवोस्तु वः।।

(*yattatva – prakaṭīkṛitau atitarām Vēdōpi nālam yataḥ*
stityutpatti–layāḥ samastajagatām yan manvatē yōginaḥ,

sākshāt–namra–surēndrabṛindamakuṭa vyālīna – ratnāvaḷī,
sōnāmśu - vraja rañjitāṅgri – yugalaḥ bhūtyai Śivōstu vaḥ).[28]

REFERENCES

1. Nilakanta Sastri, K.A., The Koḍumbāḷūr Inscription of Vikrama-Kēsarī, *J.O.R.*, Vol. VII, pp.1-10.
2. Subrahmanya Aiyer, K.V., *'Historical Sketches of the Ancient Dekhan'*, Coimbatore, 1967, Vol. II, p.194 ff.
3. *S.I.I.*, Vol. II, No. 76, pp. 382-385.
4. *E.I.*, Vol. III, No.13, pp. 75-77.
5. *A.R.E.*, 482 of 1908.
6. *A.R.E.*, 544 of 1902.
7. *A.R.E.*, 369, 370 and 371 of 1925.
8. *A.R.E.*, 117 of 1934-35.
9. *A.R.E.*, 247 of 1941-42.
10. S.S. Janaki, *Gadyakarṇāmṛta*, Madras, 1981, p. 12; *A.R.E.* 207 and 209 of 1938-39.
11. *A.R.E.*, 371 of 1925.
12. S.S. Janaki, *op.cit.*, p.23.
13. *A.R.E.*, 51 and 52 of 1892; S.S. Janaki, *op.cit.*
14. *A.R.E.*, 312 of 1954-55; S.S. Janaki, *op.cit.*, p. 23.
15. *E.I.*, Vol. IV, No.18, pp. 148-52.
16. *Ibid.*, No.17, pp. 145-148.
17. *E.I.*, Vol. VIII, No. 2, pp. 8-9.
18. *E.I.*, Vol. III, No.12-13, p. 71.
19. *Ibid.*, No.12-A, p. 70.
20. K.A. Nilakanta Sastri, *op.cit.*, v. 7, p. 9.
21. *S.I.I.*, Vol. II, No.76, v. 22, p. 384.
22. *Ibid.*, v. 23.
23. *S.I.I.*, Vol. VIII, No.135, pp. 63-64.
24. *Ibid.*
25. *S.I.I.*, Vol. II, No. 76, v.1, p. 382.

26. *E.I.*, Vol. III, No. 13, v. 2, p. 75.

    (According to the learned editor of this inscription, the meaning apparently is that Nārāyaṇa (Vishṇu), when worshipped by the Gods and asuras, grants the nectar of immortality, even more readily and abundantly than was the case at the churning of the ocean by means of the mountain Mandara).
27. *S.I.I.*, Vol. II, No. 76, v. 2, p. 382.
28. *E.I.*, Vol. III, No. 13, v.1, p. 75.

Bibliography

Epigraphical Sources

Annual Reports on Epigraphy.

Epigraphia Indica.

Pallavar Cheppeṭukal Muppatu (Thirty Pallava Copper plates), Tamil.

Varalatru Kazhagam, Madras, 1967.

Pāṇḍiyur Cheppedukal Pattu (Ten Pāṇḍyan of copper-plates), Tamil.

Varalatru Kazhagam, Madras, 1967.

South Indian Temple Inscriptions.

Travancore Archaeological Series.

Literary Sources

Bāṇa's *Kādambari,* Edited by M.R. Kale, Delhi, 1968.

King Mahendravarman's Plays: The Farce of the Pious Courtesan.

(*Bhagavad-Ajjuka Prahasanam*) and *A Farce of Druken Sport (Matta-Vilāsa-Prahasanam)* (Edited and Translated) by Michael Lockwood and A. Vishnu Bhat.

Mahābhārata, Translation by M.N. Dutt, Calcutta, 1964.

Mattavilāsaprahasana, Edited by N.P. Unni, Trivandrum, 1974.

Mēghadūta (text and translation) by M.R. Kale, Delhi, 1991.

Raghuvaṁśa Mahākāvya, Edited by V. Venkataraghava-chariar, Madras, 1991.

Śrīmad Bhāgvata, Translation by Swami Tapasyananda, Madras, 1982.

Śrīmad Vālmīki Rāmāyaṇam Edited by Amarendra Lakshamana Gargil, Pune, 1982.

Śrīmad Vālmīki Rāmāyaṇam, Edited by Kuppuswami Sastrigal, Madras, 1958.

The Abijñānaśakuntalam of Kālidāsa. Translation by M.R. Kale, Delhi, 1994.

The Raghuvamśa of Kālīdāsa, (Cantos-I-V) Translations by M.R. Kale, Bombay, 1925.

Secondary Sources

Chakravorti, Madhavadasa, *A Short History of Sanskrit Literature,* New Delhi, 1978.

Dange, Sadashiv Ambadas, *Encyclopaedia of Puranic Beliefs and Practices,* New Delhi, 1986.

Gopalan, R., *History of the Pallavas of Kanchi,* Madras, 1928.

Janaki, S.S., *Godyakarṇamṛta,* Madras, 1981.

Kane, P.V., *History of Sanskrit Poetics,* Delhi, 1961.

Keith, A.B., *History of Sanskrit Literature,* Delhi, 1996.

Krishnan, K.G., *Karandai Tamil Sangam Plates of Rājēndrachōḷa I,* New Delhi, 1984.

Macdonell, A.A., *A History of Sanskrit Literature,* Delhi, 1979.

Madhavan, Chithra, *Sanskrit Inscriptions of Tamil Nadu* (A Historical and Cultural Study (upto c. 1310 A.D.) New Delhi, 2005.

Mahalingam, T.V., *Inscriptions of the Pallava,* New Delhi, 1988.

______, *Kāñchīpuram in Early South Indian History,* Bombay, 1968.

Mani, Vettam, *Puranic Encyclopaedia*, New Delhi, 1998.

Minakshi, C., *Administration and Social Life Under the Pallavas*, Madras, 1977.

Nagaswami, R. , *Tiruttani and Velanjeri Plates*, Madras, 1979.

——, *Studies in Ancient Tamil Law and Society*, Madras, 1978.

Nilakanta Sastri, K.A., *The Cōḷas*, Madras, 1984.

——, *The Pandyan Kingdom* (From the Earliest Times to the Sixteenth century), Madras, 1972.

——, *A History of South India*, Madras, 1988.

Raman, K.V., *Sri Varadarājasvāmi Temple, Kāñchīpuram*, New Delhi, 1975.

——, *History of the Pāṇḍyas* (Tamil), Madras, 1977.

Sircar, D.C., *Indian Epigraphy*, Delhi, 1965.

Sivaramamurti, C., *Epigraphical Echoes of Kalidasa*, 1944.

——, Indian Epigraphy and South Indian Scripts, *Bulletin of Madras, Government Museum*, Vol. III, No. 4, Madras, 1966.

Subrahmaniyam Aiyar, K.V., *Historical Sketches of the Ancient Dekhan*, Coimbatore, 1967, Vol. II.

Swaminathan, S., *The Early Chōḷas* (History, Art and Culture), Delhi, 1998.

Venkatakrishna Rao, *A Hand book of Classical Sanakrit Literature*, New Delhi, 1961.

Venkataraman, K.R, *Hoysalas in the Tamil Country* (12th-14th centuries), Annamalainagar, 1950.

Winternitz, M., *History of Indian Literature*, Delhi, 1974.

Articles

Buhler, G., The Indian Inscriptions and the Antiquity of Indian Artificial Potery, *I.A.* (Feb., 1913), pp. 29-32, pp. 137-148, 172-179, 188-193 and 230-249.

Diskalkar D.B., Dravidion or South Indian Inscriptions, *J.I.H.*, Vol. XXXIV, pp. 173-182.

Krishan, K.G., Sanskrit in Inscriptions of Tamilnadu, from *Savasti Sri* (Chabbra Felicitation Volume), New Delhi, 1984.

Mahalingam, T.V., The Bāṇas in South Indian History, *J.I.H.*, Vol. XXIX (1951), pp. 153-181 and 277 to 305.

Nagaswamy, R., Mahēndra's Inscription at Tiruchirapalli—A Study, *J.O.R.*, Vol. VII, pp. 135-138.

Nagaswamy, R., *Bulletin De 1'Ecole Francaise (D'Extereme Orient)* Tome LXXXVI, Paris, 1987.

Narasimhachar, R., Bamaha and Dandi, *I.A.* (April 1912) Vol. XXXXI, pp. 90-93.

Nilakanta Sastri, K.A., The Kodumbāḷūr Inscription of Vikrama-Kēari, *J.O.R.*, Vol. VII, pp. 1-10.

____, Sanskrit Learning in the Cola Empire, *J.O.R.*, Vol. IX, Part I, 1937, pp. 1-10.

Pillay, K.K., Dalavaypuram Plates of Parāntaka Vīranāyaṇa, *J.O.R.*, Vol. VII, pp. 159-165.

Raghvan, V., Sanskrit and Epigraphy, *The Mysore Orientalist*, Vol. IV, (No. 1), March, 1971, pp. 1-7.

Ramachandran, T.N., The Royal Artist, Mahedravarman I, *J.O.R.*, Vol. VII, pp. 219-245 and 303 ff.

Sircar, D.C., South Indian Epigraphy Its Value as Source Material in South Indian Studies, *Dr. T.V. Mahalingam Commenmoration Volume*, Mysore, 1990, pp. 183-190.

Sankaranarayanan, S., A Pallava Inscriptional Poem in Sanskrit, *ALB*, Vol. 55, 1991, pp. 71-90.

Sankaranarayanan, S., Sanskrit Education in Ancient Tamil Country (An Epigraphical Survey), *ALB*, Vol. 57, 1993 pp. 7-33.

Srinivasan, P.R., Gangādharāshṭakam in Pallava Inscription from Tiruchirapalli from '*Srinidhiḥ-Perspective in Indian Archaeology, Art and Culture.* (Shri K.R. Srinivasam Festschrift), pp. 431-435.

Subramaniam, T.N., The Paḷḷankovil Jaina Copper-Plate Grant of Early Pallava period, *TASSI*, Vol. IV (1958-59), pp. 41-83.

______, The Dalavāypuram Copper-Plate Grant of Parāntaka Vīra-Nārāyaṇa Pāṇḍya *TASSI* (1962-65), pp. 1-31.

Subramaniam, T.N. and Srinivasan, P.R., The Śivakāsī Copper-Plate Grant of Vīra-Pāṇḍya, *TASSI* (1962-65), pp. 33-52.

Subramaniam, V.S., Characteristic Features of Sanskrit Inscriptions From South Indian Studies, *Dr. T.V. Mahalingam Commemoration Volume*, Mysore, 1990, pp. 191-205.

Index